All Sketched Out

by

Steve Connellan

Copyright © 2021 Steve Connellan

All rights reserved.

ISBN:9798520366799

DEDICATION

Dedicated to New Zealand which has provided such a wealth of beautiful scenery and a country our family can now call home.

CONTENTS

The contents of this book are based on sketch books that I have kept on my travels in the UK and New Zealand. In addition, there is comment on local history attached to each sketch.

In this update I have also added some watercolours and oil paintings which, although still plein air, are on watercolour paper or canvas as opposed to sketch books.

All of the paintings in the last 8 years have been in New Zealand.

Any errors in historical commentary are entirely my fault.

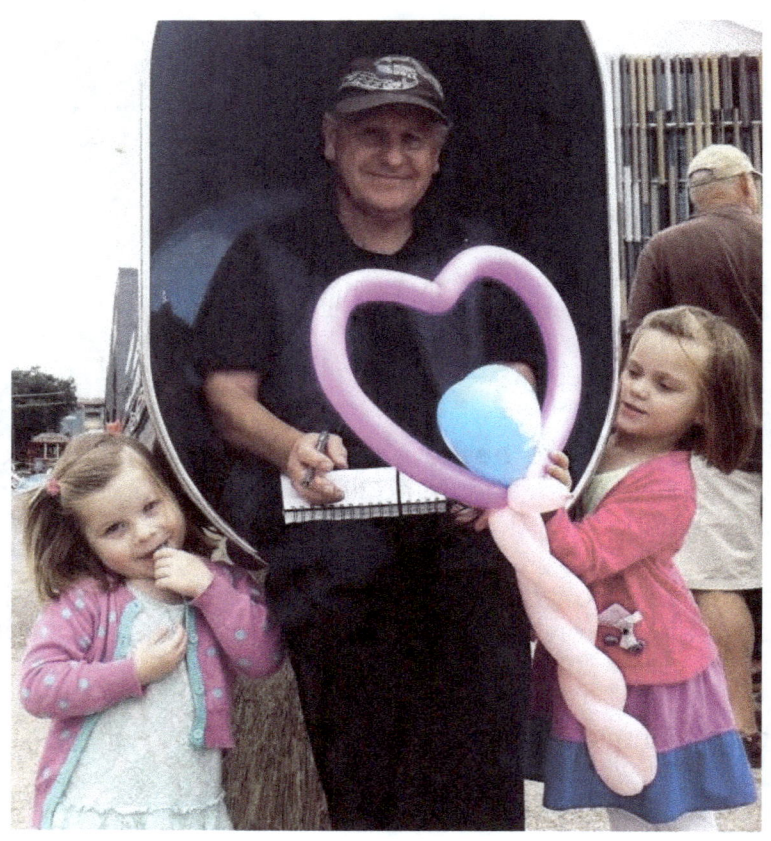

Sketching at Wynyard Quarter with Jessica and Emily.

ACKNOWLEDGEMENTS

I would like to acknowledge my wife who has put up with me tripping off to various sites to doodle away the day and the passers-by who have encouraged me while sketching en plein air. Their interest in my work and positive feedback has helped me overcome my earlier lack of confidence in putting myself out there for all to see.

Others who have maintained my enthusiasm are Sue Goodchild who taught me that a sketch book could become a prized personal possession and Jennifer Cruden of Plein Air Painters of NZ whose artistry and organisational skills have encouraged me and many others to get out there in all weathers and put paint on canvas.

Sue Goodchild

http://www.gallerygoodchild.com/

Plein Air Painters–New Zealand

https://www.meetup.com/AucklandPleinAirPainters-NewZealand/

Introduction

It was July 2007 and I had just retired from my post as a hospital consultant. A major milestone in anyone's life and apart from continuing with some private medicine I now had a lot more time on my hands which needed to be occupied whilst avoiding getting under my wife's feet. I suspect it was quite a major milestone in her life, suddenly having me at home during the day. However, she had a cunning plan to help me and her cope with this transition and shortly after, I was on my way to France for a week's painting holiday. I had always enjoyed drawing and I think that element of biology in school was probably part of the reason I started to be interested in the human body and its workings. A lot of my subsequent revision for exams was helped by doodling and producing full page cartoons which I used as aides memoire. This is from the back of one of my old revision notebooks, reminding me of the hazards of excess alcohol!

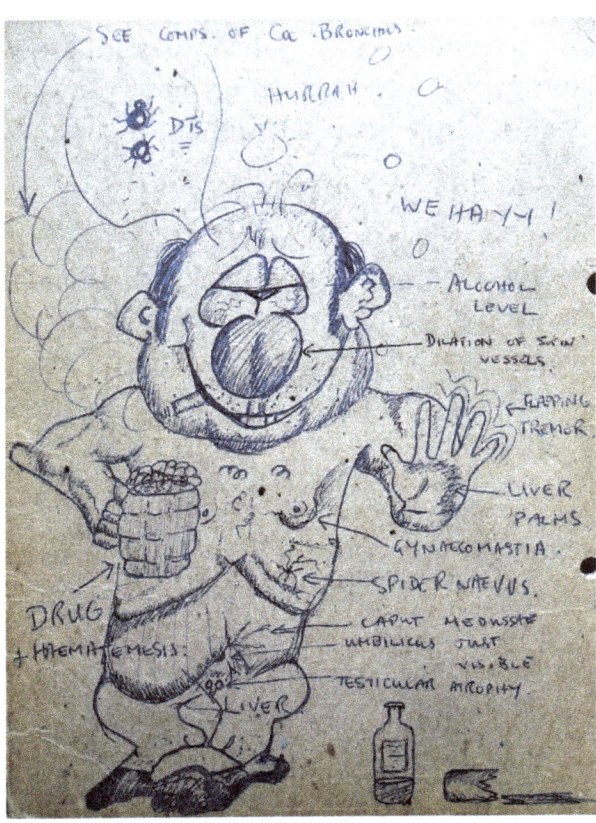

The French Influence

My destination was Le Petit Bois Gleu at Renazé in the Loire region. Sue Goodchild and her husband Paul, with her as the tutor and Paul as the chef, had renovated an old farmhouse and catered for artist holidays.

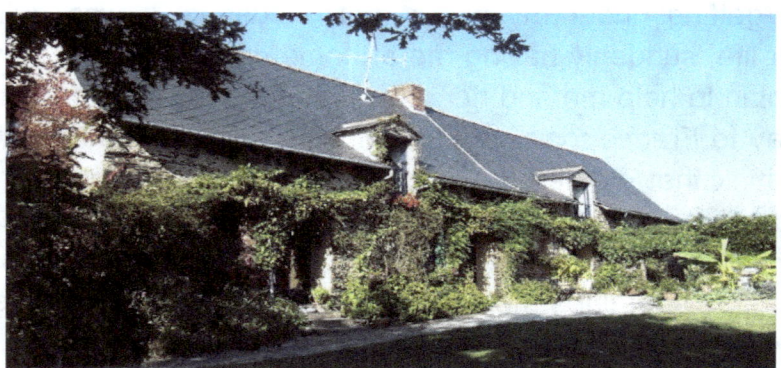

It was an idyllic week with summer weather and a patient teacher who inspired us all. We would be taken out to picturesque countryside, left to find our own view and, while we worked, a large table with lunch and wine would be set up close by in the shade.

Sue was very keen on sketching (pen and wash) and encouraged us to sit at a market and do rapid sketches of groups of people, to get accustomed to catching a moment on paper. She would keep large sketch books, full of local scenes produced on holidays. I could see why these would bring back strong memories of places visited which would probably last longer and remain more accessible than the average photo stored away on some laptop or 'cloud' facility.

I will always remember her anecdote of sitting in a market with only a watercolour brush and serviette and using the coffee grounds from her cup to produce a sketch of sepia shade and light. Her advice was to always get a feeling if a group were likely to stay in one spot for a while and with experience it was quite easy to tell, by their body language, whether they were likely to stick around for your sketching. Also to concentrate on their upper bodies and shoulders first, adding heads later. One of my earliest attempts at rapid sketching was at Renazé market where I took a chance that the woman bending forward to write a cheque would take her time!

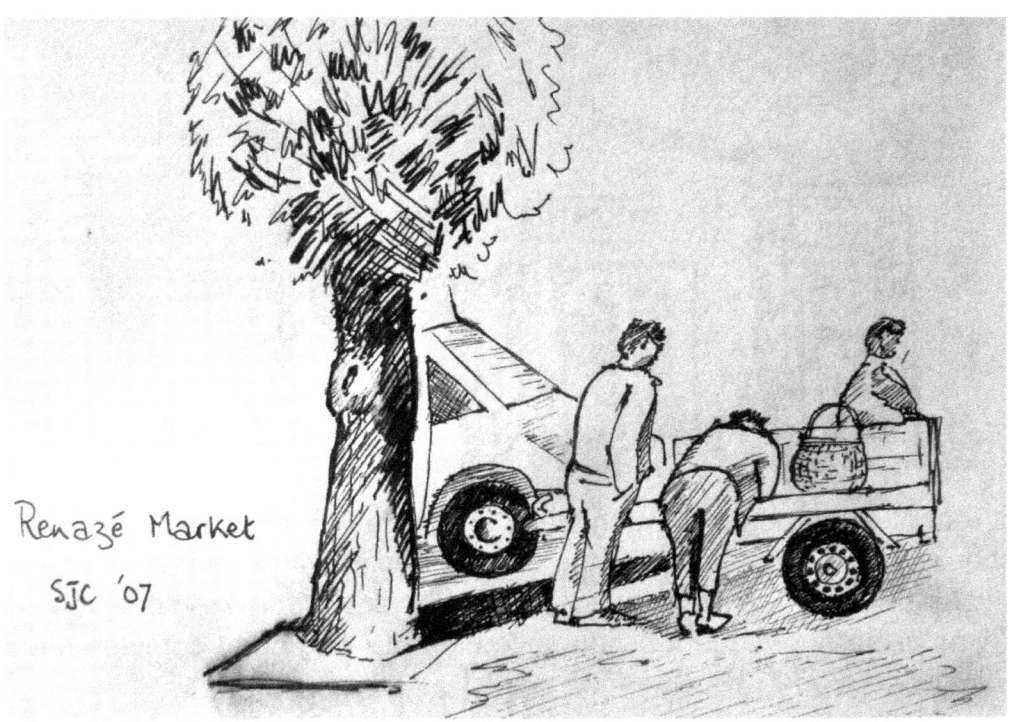

Another interesting exercise would happen every morning at the start of our sessions. This would entail finding an object of interest, concentrating on it for a full minute and then getting back to the studio and reproducing it accurately.

I soon learnt that there was always some detail that had not made its way into my consciousness. We were allowed to return for a further 30 seconds and then to finally compare our drawing with the original object. Quite an insight into the potential for training the mind to recall small detail.

Another source of subjects was their pet St Bernard puppy, Belle, and a goose called Geiger. Belle was very wary of Geiger and seemed constantly concerned that Geiger would steal her bone.

The following quick sketch illustrates that anxious look over the shoulder that Belle would make as Geiger slowly padded by!

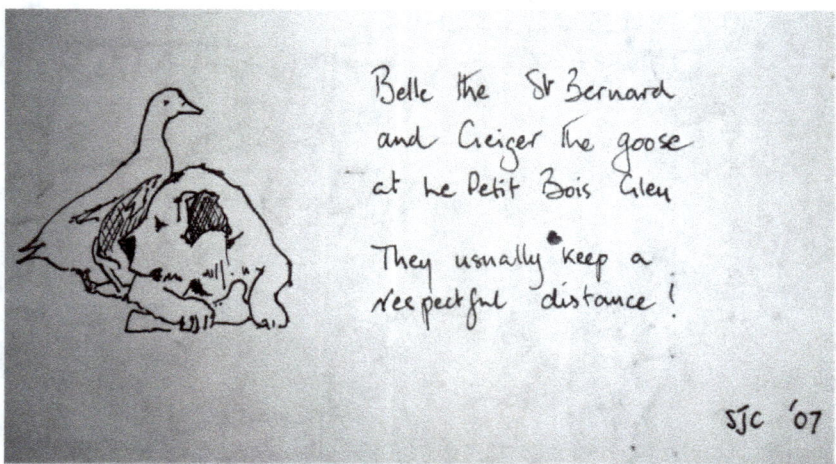

My first real plein air pen and wash was my picture of their old well, which had a lot of character. Having completed the original pen drawing, with what I assumed was a water resistant ink, I started to apply the watercolour wash only to find that the ink was dissolving! Urgent action saved the drawing and I completed it using watercolour pencils.

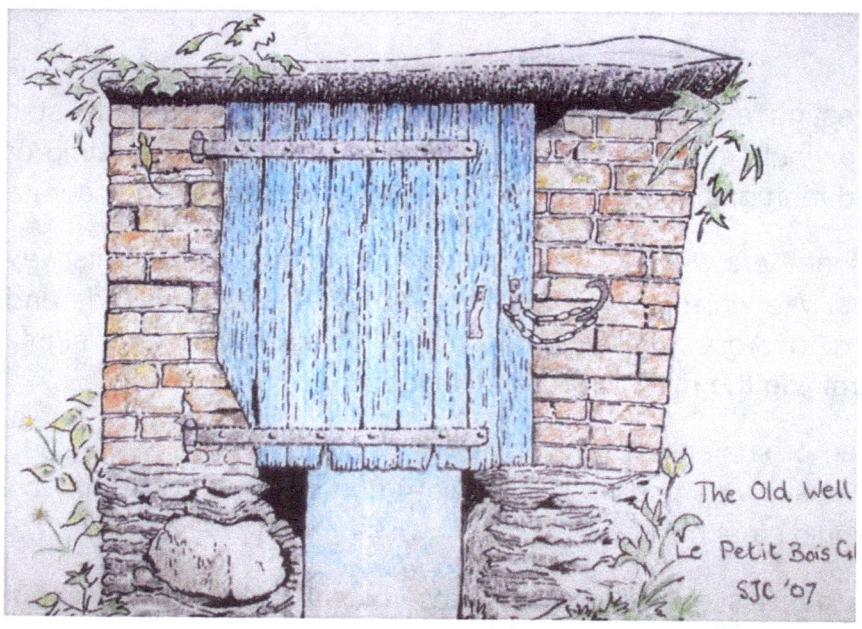

And so I returned from France with a lot of enthusiasm for sketching and painting in watercolours. I soon had a sketch book, which in retrospect was probably more suited to just sketching, without adding any wash, as the paper would tend to warp with the addition of water! All the result of naivety in my new art form. However, I stuck with this book and completed the last page after 8 years of entries.

There has been a gradual transition from simple quick sketches without colour to more obsessional pen and wash with lots of detail. During this transition I discovered oil painting, although a lot of my plein air work has tended to be on 6 x 9 inch canvas board with a preliminary sketch. So my brushes have tended to be small and the finished product more realism than impressionist.

Another reason for the final product to be more realistic than impressionistic was the fact that I had also had cataract surgery on both eyes. I could see for miles!

This book aims to link my work with anecdotes and local facts (historical or otherwise) about the scenery I was presented with both in the UK and New Zealand. We now have an extended Kiwi family (with grandchildren) and love our life here in New Zealand.

Grandson Finn now has a brother Archer. All of the grandkids seem to love drawing and painting and it will be interesting to see how their individual talents mature over time.

My family have always encouraged me to maintain my enthusiasm for art and this book which now includes the more recent update is really for them as a memento of some of the places and experiences we have shared. It will also take me back to many idyllic sessions of doodling away the day in beautiful surroundings. My form of therapeutic meditation!

The following section covers some earlier travel within Europe prior to being established more permanently in New Zealand.

Northern Hemisphere

I've already covered some of my early sketching while in France and, although retired, I was still invited to specialist medical conferences abroad. This took me to Stockholm in 2007 and with a somewhat more relaxed approach to medical education I took my sketchbook with me and spent an afternoon sitting with my back to City Hall, (the venue for the Nobel Prize banquet), sketching the view across the river to Riddarholmen, which is a small island that forms part of the old town. It was originally used for grazing goats but now houses a number of private palaces and the royal burial church for a number of Swedish monarchs. The tip of my pen was broader than I would use now and there was no inclination to add colour at this stage.

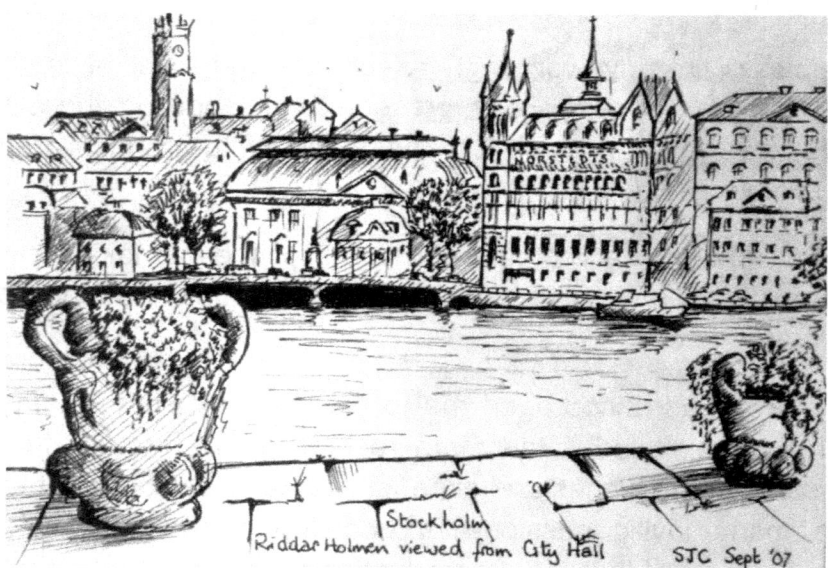

A month later, back in our UK home, I set off for a walk down Brewood canal and found a shaded spot with bench provided. I learnt later from a friend that the narrow boat on the right was the permanent home of a lady and her dogs.

This sketch will always remind me of walks down the Brewood canal towpath which was a great way to experience all the changing seasons.

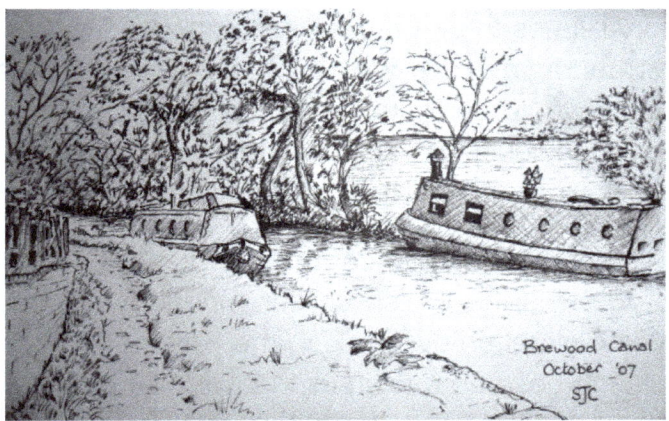

Brewood in South Staffordshire was our home for 25 years and we lived in a renovated wood worker's cottage next to Chillington estate.

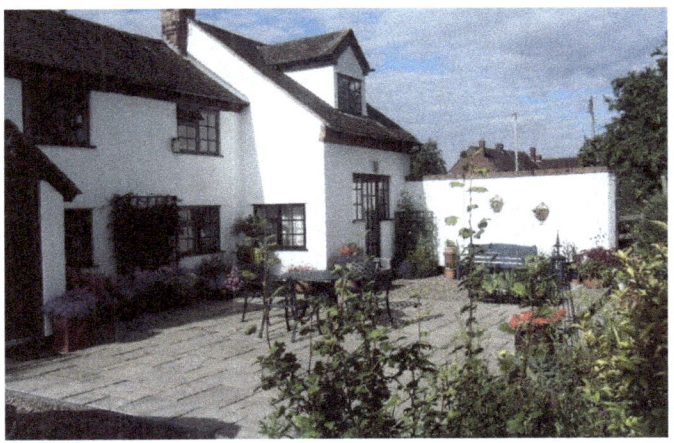

The village probably originated in Anglo-Saxon times and the origin of its name is thought to be, 'Wood on the Hill'. The history of Brewood constitutes a substantial book in its own right (David Horovitz, Brewood, 1988 ISBN 1-85421-011-4) and will not be covered here. Brewood canal (Shropshire Union Canal) was opened in 1843 and runs through the parish north to south and there is a wharf where narrow boats can be hired. It was said that the 'Bargees' who ran the working narrow boats, years ago, would stop off at the Bridge Inn, get roaring drunk and terrorise the villagers! The canal tow path provides lovely country walks.

One more poignant memory relates to an unfortunate man who lived on a narrow boat in Brewood and was under my care with pancreatic cancer. He stoically accepted his diagnosis and I would do 'houseboat visits' to check his symptom control from time to time. He would travel down the canal to visit Compton Hospice for support; so his life remained strongly connected to his canal home.

Living on the fringe of the West Midlands offered easy access to open countryside extending out towards the Welsh border. Bridgnorth is one of those towns with a great history and situation overlooking the Severn River as it makes it way south through a valley. It became a town in 1101 and its castle was built to defend against Welsh attacks. The town is split into 'High' and 'Low Town' depending on its relationship to the river. The view from High Town down to the river provides some dramatic scenery and by this time I had progressed to the addition of watercolour wash.

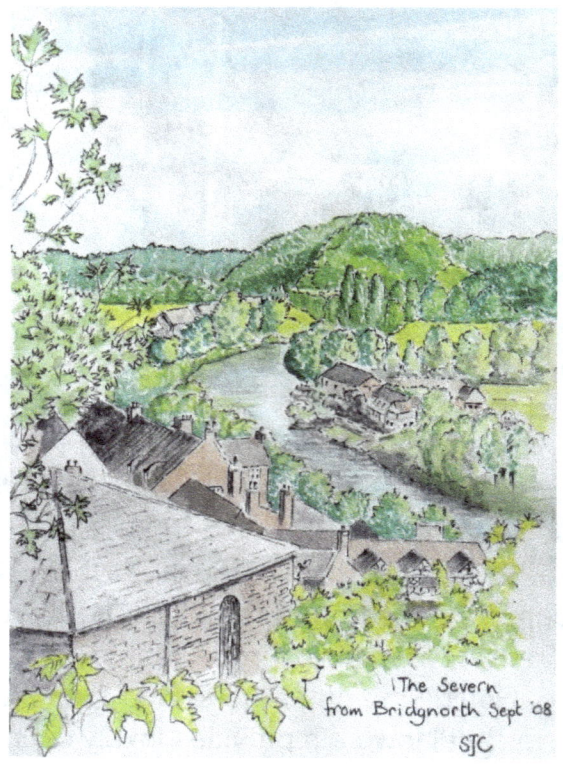

The Severn from Bridgnorth Sept '08
SJC

Southern Hemisphere

By 2008 we were travelling back and forward from the UK to New Zealand to visit family and I would take every opportunity to add to my sketchbook. This rapid sketch, while waiting for a bus on Queen Street, Auckland, was just about completed in time as the bus arrived!

This view is up Vulcan Lane, off Queen Street. The Occidental Hotel was frequented by printers and journalists in the mid-19th century and the lane was nick-named Vultures Lane when it became popular with prostitutes, peddlers, bookmakers and cockfights. It was subsequently named Vulcan Street after the Vulcan Forge.

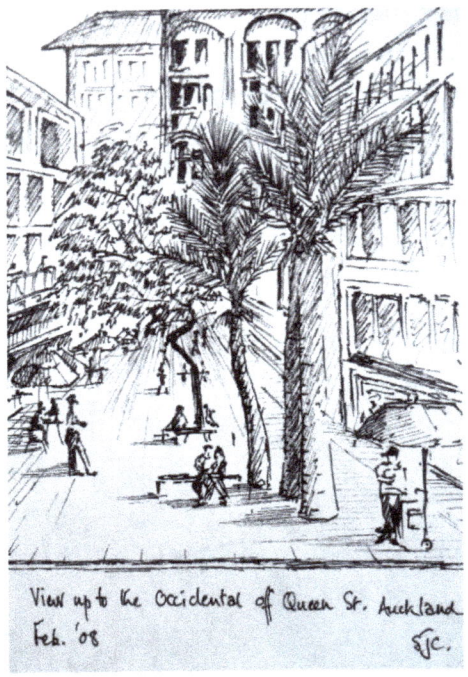

I would often walk down to Westhaven and with Harbour Bridge on my left and my back to the Royal New Zealand Yacht Squadron, I had a great view of the harbour.

The following pen and wash uses a bit of artistic license as I have condensed the view somewhat to squash in Devonport on the right.

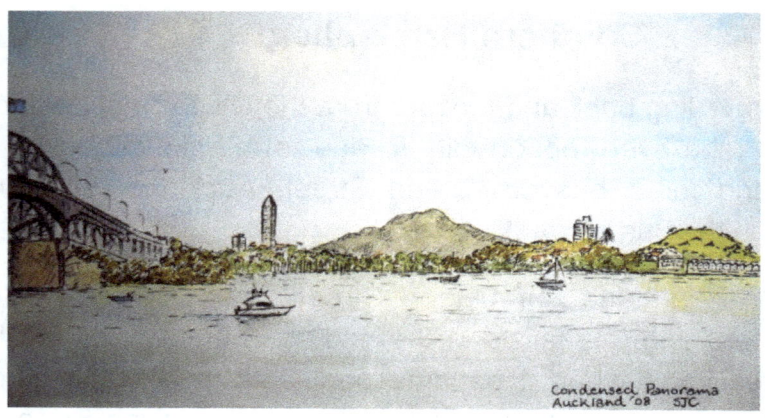

This further condensed scene is from Meola Reef and provides a view from the other side of the harbour bridge with Rangitoto (dormant volcano) and Sky Tower in the background. More about these later. Meola Reef is now a popular place for dog walking. It actually extends about 2 kilometres across the harbour and was formed some 28,000 years ago from the advancing edge of lava flow that originated from Mount St John volcano. Mangroves have covered the area close to shore but the original lava can still be seen, especially at lower tides.

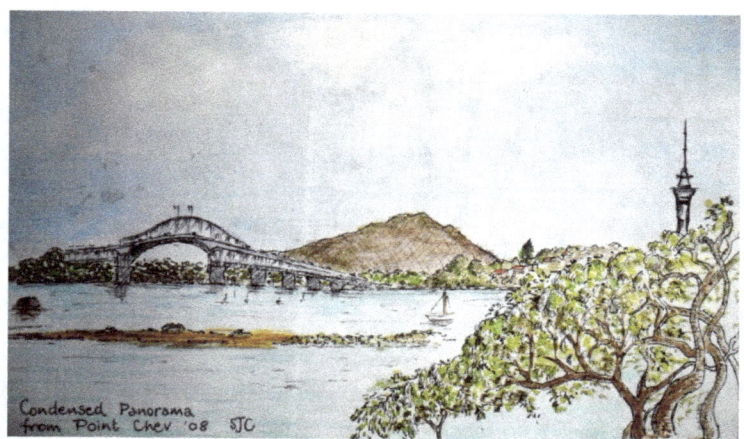

I found this nice quote in the Encyclopaedia of New Zealand, from the autobiography of historian Sir Keith Sinclair, in which he describes playing on Meola Reef.

" ... It was treacherous with crevices in the black basalt rock. But it was also alive with mussels, oysters, crabs, pools of shrimps and tommy-cod ... Once out on the reef we would often light a fire and bake potatoes, wrapped in mud, in the embers ... There were edible shellfish too, including scallops to be picked up during exceptionally low tides. The Swiss Family Robinson had nothing on us."

My son Mike and daughter-in-law Mareesa occasionally walked their Beagle Bess on the reef.

We travel up to the East coast of North Island on occasions and one of our trips back in 2008 was to a Homestay (B & B) at Parua Bay near Whangerei. By the mid-19th century there were four European families established in a small settlement on the western side of this bay. This was at a time in New Zealand of considerable conflict between the immigrant Europeans (Pākehā) and the indigenous Māori. The government of the time purchased 10,000 acres at Parua in 1858. It was possible under the 'Forty Acre Scheme' for any settler to acquire 40 acres provided they were over 18 years and agreed to certain conditions.

I completed this pen and wash from the sitting room of our hosts, so not quite plein air but what a magnificent vista from their panoramic window!

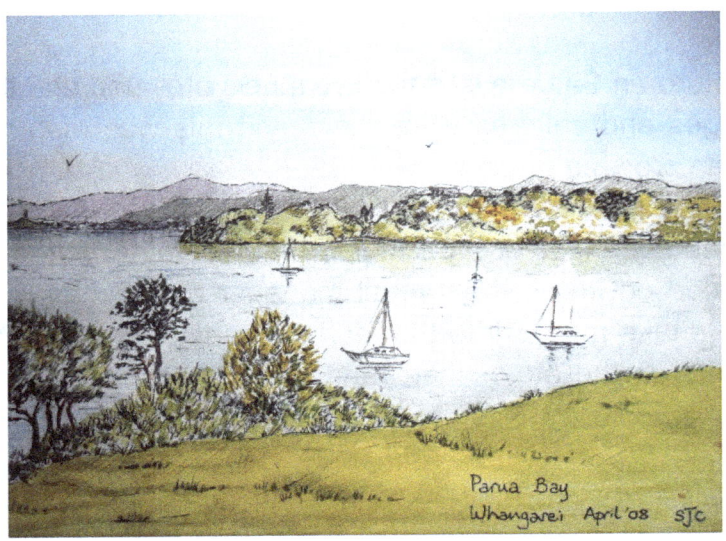

A favourite destination is Matakana, near Warkworth. A river of the same name flows through the town and on to Kawau Bay. It is well known for its farmers' market, cinema, fine restaurants, book and food shops. The Morrison and James pottery, Ascension Vineyard and Charlie's for excellent ice cream, are all part of a great mix. Before any Europeans arrived, there were Māori settlements at Tāwharanui, Omaha and Mahurangi. In 1841 a large section of land was bought from the Hauraki tribes. Prior to that there were a few Europeans who had negotiated the right to reside with local iwi. Early settlers were also in lower Matakana, at the river mouth (Sandspit), but started to move up river to where the timber resources were, in what is now Matakana Village. Flax was also harvested from this area. By 1880, fruit became an important industry and this gave way to farming by 1900. A number of vineyards have originated from these farms. Another resource in the area, still in use, is clay. It was used in earlier times to produce bricks at a factory in Brick Bay but from 1978 it has supplied the Morris and James pottery.

In April 2008 I sat at the edge of the market to sketch. This rustic market square is right on the river's edge and all the food is presented by the local producers. One great feature is the variety of food for sale and the wafting of various delicious smells around the site along with the ever present coffee aroma.

Another nice feature on Saturdays is the live music provided and this day was no exception. All ages and cultures were there and this was also reflected in the very cosmopolitan produce on offer.

I noticed someone peering over my shoulder at one stage and he started to chat with me. He turned out to be the overall manager of the market. The following sketch will always take me back to that early experience of the market, listening to the band, taking in the atmosphere and smells and having a lazy sketching hour.

As short drive will take you past Ascension Vineyard to the beautiful Omaha beach.

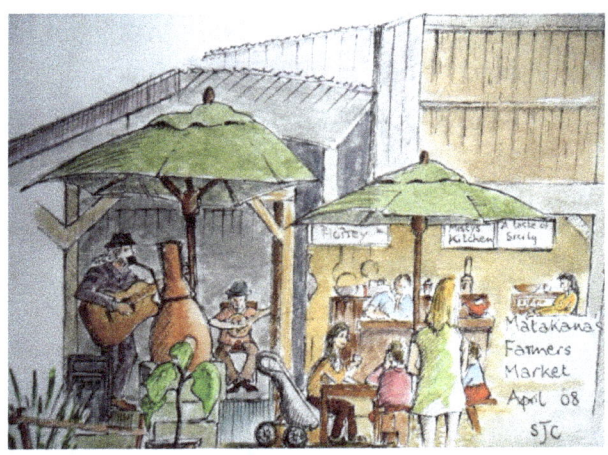

Another new experience, since emigrating, has been fishing. My son-in-law (Darren) has his own 'Tinny' (aluminium hulled boat) and I have had the opportunity to travel out with him to the waters around the harbour, Rangitoto channel or towards the island of Waiheke. He has introduced me to fishing for Snapper, drifting with soft bait or anchored up with Squid, Pilchard, Mullet, Yellow Tail or other bait fish on the hook. Although not sketching from real life this time, the following is my only attempt at a self-portrait taken from a photo when I caught my first Snapper.

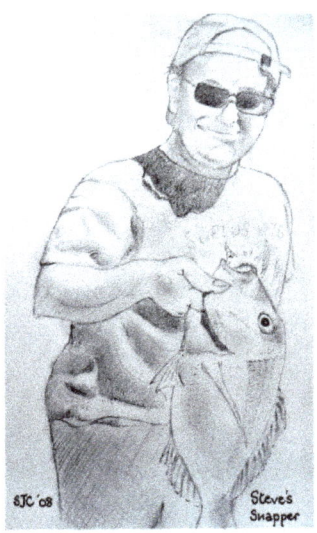

While staying at a bach, with the family in 2009, we went out from Omaha and I had an extraordinary lucky catch of four different species with the same tackle. This stimulated the pen and wash below, recalling the Snapper, John Dory, Skipjack Tuna and Trevally all caught that same day. We had sashimi Tuna and pan fried Snapper that night!

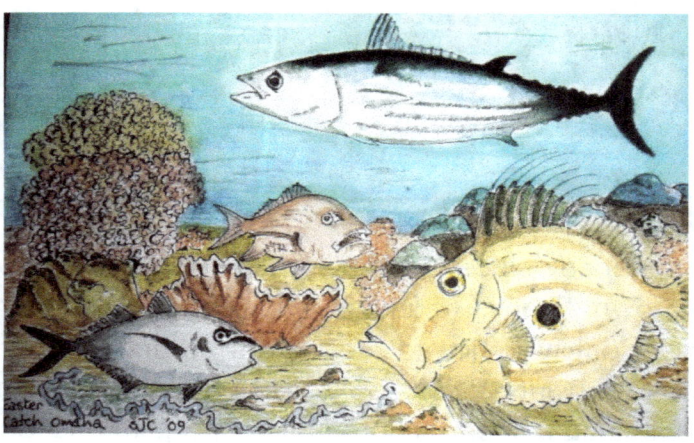

In 2009, Team New Zealand took part in the Louis Vuitton Pacific Series and I went down to the Viaduct area to view the various yachts taking part.

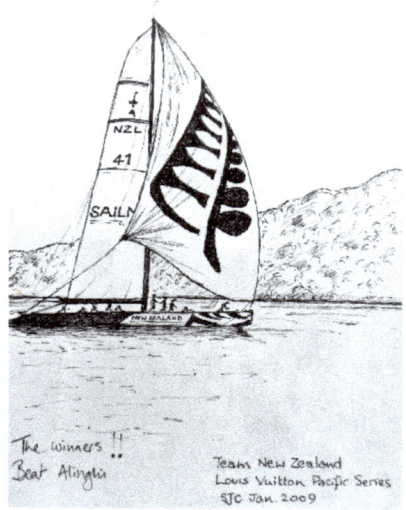

I had a good view from a seafood restaurant that had been set up alongside the harbour. While sketching from my table I noted someone tucking into some tasty looking prawn cutlets and ordered some myself. I was shocked and delighted to receive a plate full with at least three times the number of prawns.

Further enquiries from the waitress made me realise that the staff thought I was some media artist and had decided to give me special treatment in case I was also reviewing their restaurant. The one and only perk I have ever experienced while sketching!

The relevant sketch (above) was of the winning Team New Zealand yacht who beat Alinghi.

That same year my wife and I took a day trip on the Soren Larsen around the Auckland harbour.

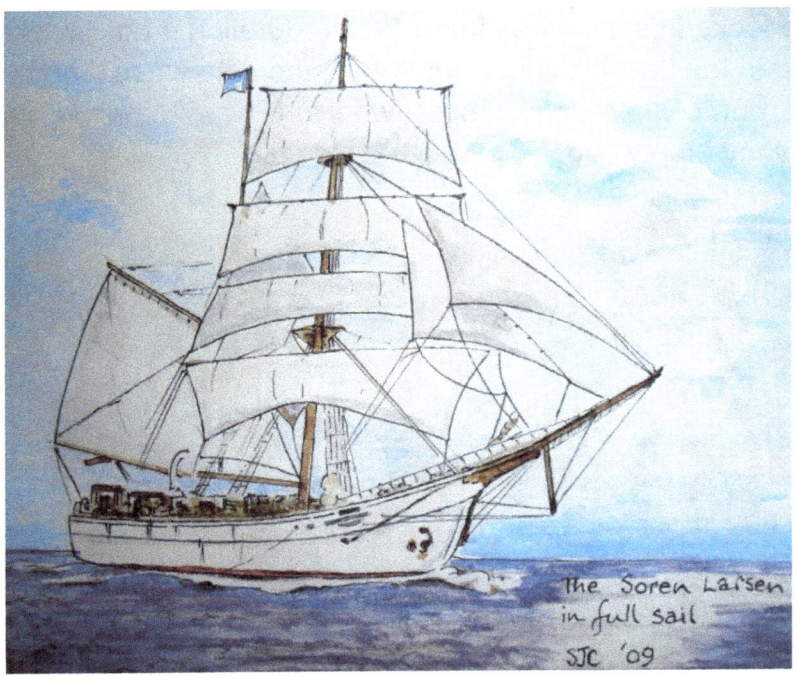

This beautiful tallship is a brigantine (defined by the number and types of sails). It was built mostly with oak and beech in 1949 in Denmark. She originally carried goods throughout Scandinavia and northern Europe but was gutted by fire in 1972. The hull was purchased six years later and the ship was resurrected as a 19th century style brigantine.

The Captain informed us that they made regular trips up to the islands and it was possible to sign on as crew. One of their regulars was a 70 year old who would happily climb up the mast rigging!

It subsequently appeared in the BBC series 'The Onedin Line', 'The French Lieutenant's Woman' and 'Shackleton'. She has been chartered for South Pacific island voyages and in 2011 was purchased by Sydney Harbour Tallships.

I would often get the Outer Link bus round to Parnell Rise where there are a number of art galleries and would have a break at what was then 'Starbucks'. This young man was very engrossed on his mobile phone and, working on the principle that he looked as if he was there for the duration, I quickly sketched him in and then filled in the background. Fortunately, the cafe wasn't too busy so they didn't kick me out of my corner spot where I was doodling for an hour accompanied by my empty cup!

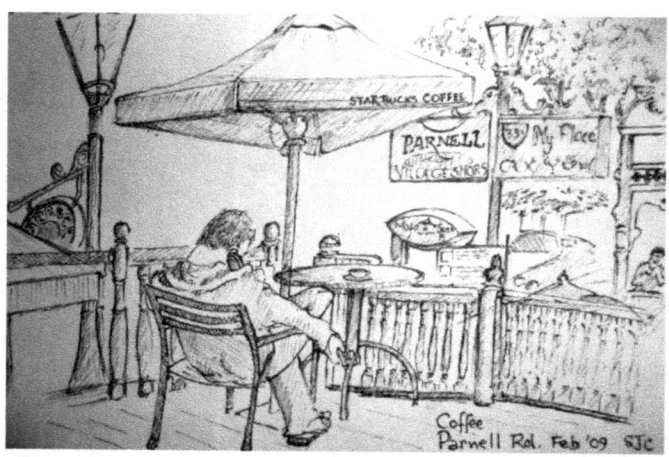

There is a bench just outside the Ponsonby Library (Leys Institute) and this provides a good spot to sit and sketch this famous landmark at the corner of 'Three Lamps'. It was at one time the Belgian Beer Cafe but its history goes back 105 years. It used to be the Ponsonby Post Office. The unfortunate postmaster, Augustus Braithwaite, was murdered in his own home by Dennis Gunn who took his keys and burgled the Post Office strong room. He was ultimately identified by finger print evidence, as these were on record following a prison term for evading military service. He was hanged 4 months after the murder.

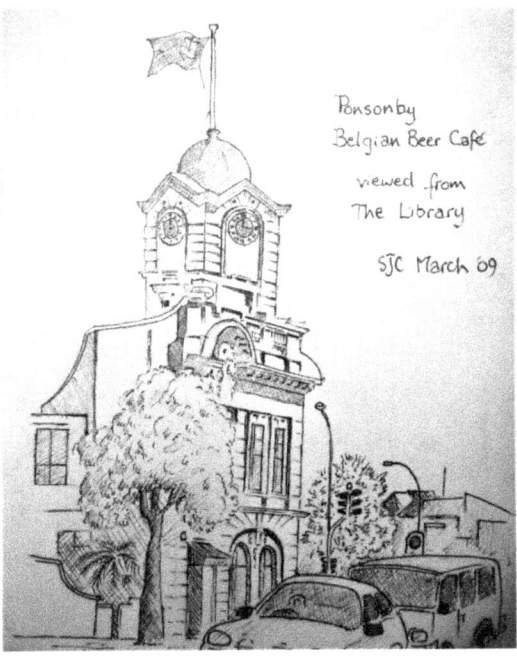

Point Chevalier beach is a short drive away from us and has had its ups and downs in popularity through the years. There used to be tramlines that ran down Point Chevalier road to the terminus at Coyle Park and this was a popular trip for those living in Grey Lynn. However, after the opening of the harbour bridge the beach was much less popular and local businesses shut down. The tramlines were removed during the 1950s. The width of Point Chevalier road and the large roundabout at Coyle Park are the reminders of the previous tramway and terminus.

The beach had to be re-sanded in 2008 because of degradation. This was achieved with 50,000 cubic metres of deepwater sand taken from the Pakiri coastline. This has rejuvenated its popularity. Large numbers of visitors descend on to Coyle Park and the adjacent Point Chevalier beach during the summer months and families gather for BBQs and their children enjoy the park.

The following view is from the east end of the beach.

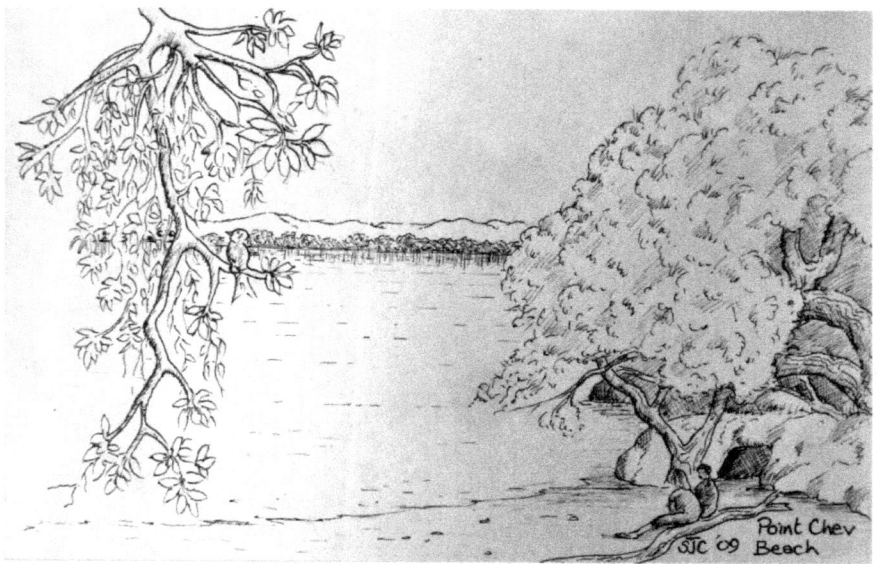

In 2009 we travelled down to South Island and visited Nelson and the Golden Bay area. The following sketch of Nelson's Farmers' Market is not one of my quick ones! I spent over an hour sketching and was fortunate to have in front of me a couple at a table and a group of men engrossed in conversation.

The basic sketch was done with water resistant pen and the watercolour wash added later. A photograph helped me to remember the various colours. This reproduction of the sketch looks a bit pinkish which I think maybe not totally true to the original.

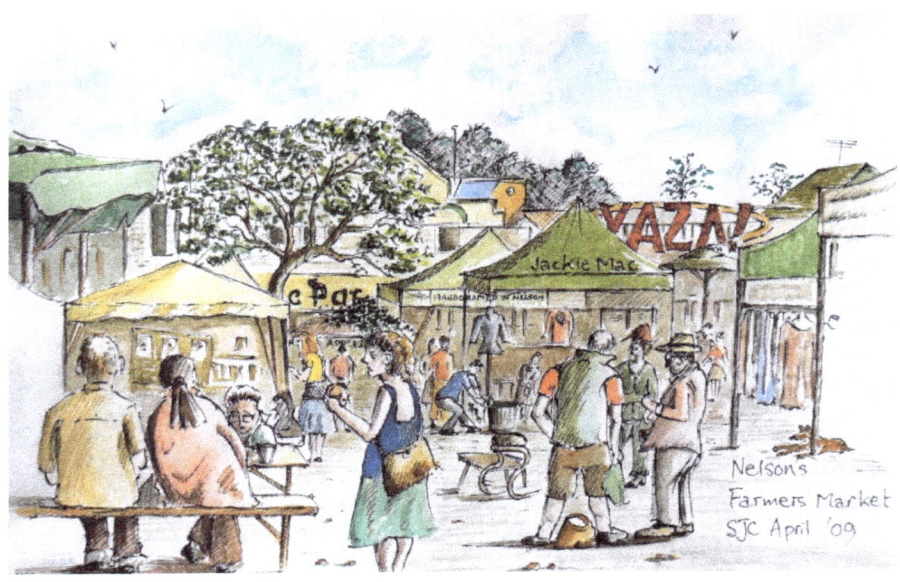

Nelson's second bishop, Andrew Suter, was a skilful painter and established a sketching club and art society. In his honour, posthumously, the Suter Gallery was opened in 1899 and became Nelson's centre for the visual arts. One of New Zealand's famous watercolourists was John Gully who emigrated from England in 1851 and lived in Nelson between 1860 - 1888. He often went on sketching trips and kept sketch books filled with pencil studies and wash drawings in sepia and colour.

We also visited Napier on the same trip and the following pen and wash is of Clive Square. Napier was devastated by the 1931 Hawke's Bay earthquake. Nearly all the buildings in the centre of Napier and Hastings were levelled and 256 people were killed. Secondary fires caused a lot of the damage and, with water mains damaged, the fire brigade were unable to save many buildings. It was possible to pump water from Clive Square to stop the fires spreading south.

The rebuilding of Napier resulted in one of the finest examples of Art Deco architecture in the world.

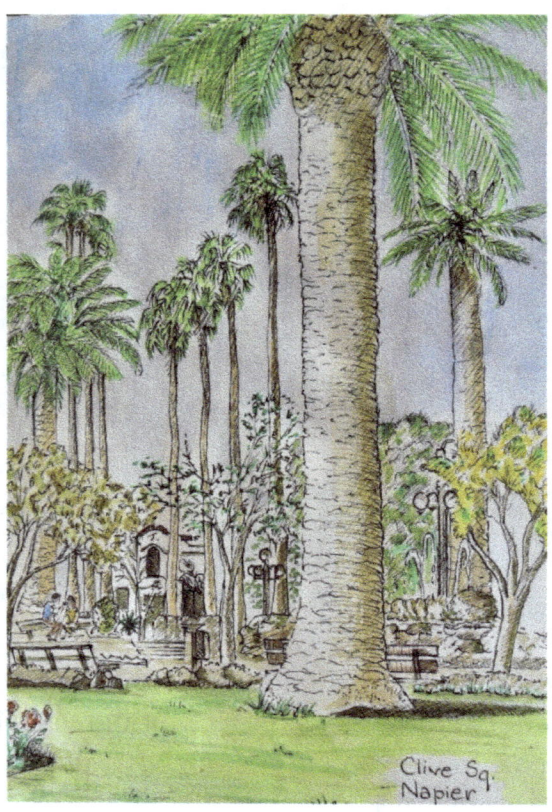

This next view is from Bastion Point, above Mission Bay, looking towards Okahu Bay and beyond to Auckland CBD. This area has been the subject of considerable unrest through the years. The land was originally occupied by Ngāti Whātua and overlooked rich fishing and farming land. In 1885, the New Zealand government built a military outpost there, in view of its strategic position overlooking the Waitematā Harbour and concerns of a Russian invasion.

When the land was no longer needed for defence in 1941 it was not returned to Māori but gifted to Auckland City Council for a reserve. In 1976 the Crown announced that it was going to sell off land to the highest bidder. From an original purchase of 3000 acres for £200 a subsequent 90 acres was sold for £24,000.

Māori were forcibly displaced from the area and moved to alternative accommodation known locally as Boot Hill. In 1977, the Orakei Māori Action Group organised occupation of the remaining Crown land (with some support from Pākehā) to prevent Robert Muldoon's government from confiscating it. They built a Marae with adjacent housing and grew crops.

The occupation lasted 507 days and was finally ended by forced eviction of a peaceful protest. Following the Orakei report of Waitangi in 1987, the land was returned to Ngāti Whātua with a $3 million dollar settlement and their corporate structure now manages the land.

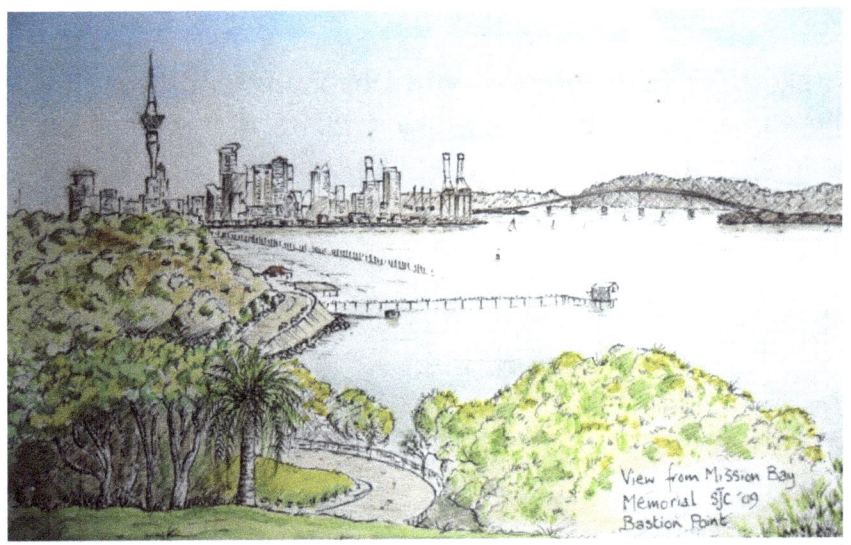

During one of my walks, around Christmas 2009, I had a rest at the Viaduct Harbour and was taken with the message which had been added to the side of the KZ1 yacht which was used to challenge for the 1988 America's Cup.

After sketching for an hour I had a tap on the shoulder and a woman, who had been watching me from one of the high rise flats behind, came down to have a look at what I was drawing.

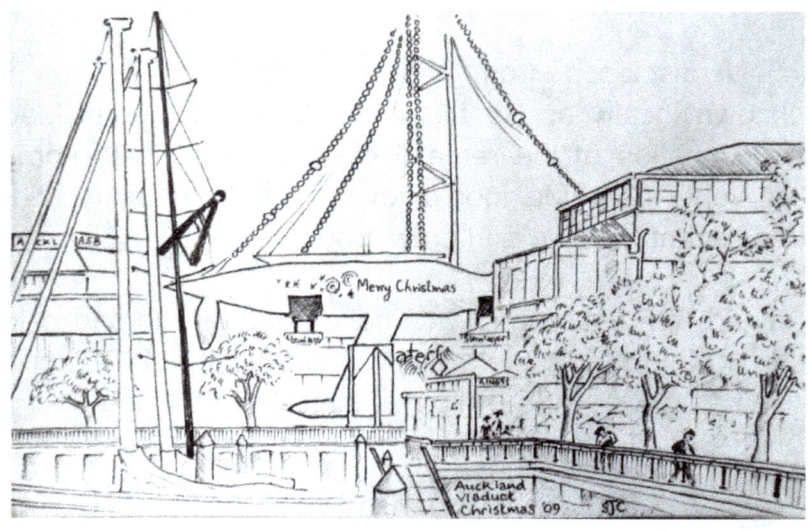

The following sketch is of Torpedo Bay in Devonport and I remember sitting in the shade with a beautiful blue January sky in 2010. At the same time there was a major thunderstorm making its way over the Auckland CBD, directly across the harbour from where I was sitting! You can see the lower reaches of North Head to the left of the picture.

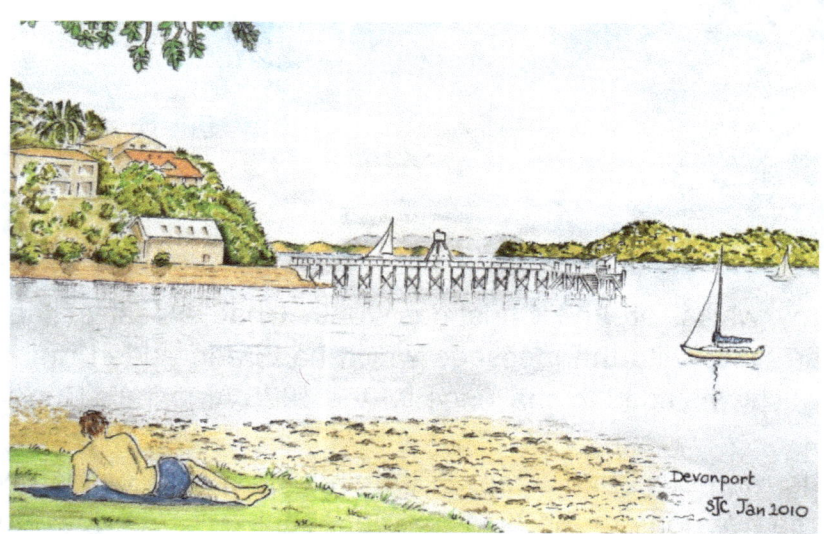

Prior to the arrival of Europeans, Māori had settled at the foot of North Head and there was a fortified settlement (pā) at nearby Mount Victoria (Takarunga). North Head (or Maungauika) was considered an excellent vantage point for defence and became an important coastal defence when it was feared that the Russian fleet was on its way. By 1885 three large gun batteries were built. Over the next 25 years, prisoners were used to rebuild the fortifications, tunnels and engine rooms. They were housed in a prison at the summit. Various additions to the fortifications followed around the times of war but by the end of the 1950s the coastal defence system was scrapped. The Navy ran a training school at the summit until 1996 and the National Museum of the Royal New Zealand Navy remains a popular attraction at the base of North Head.

On another family trip we stayed in Tairua on the Coromandel and my daughter Claire and I sat in the back garden of the bach and sketched this view overlooking the coast. The tiny yellow smudge in the sea to the left is the boat we went fishing in the day before!

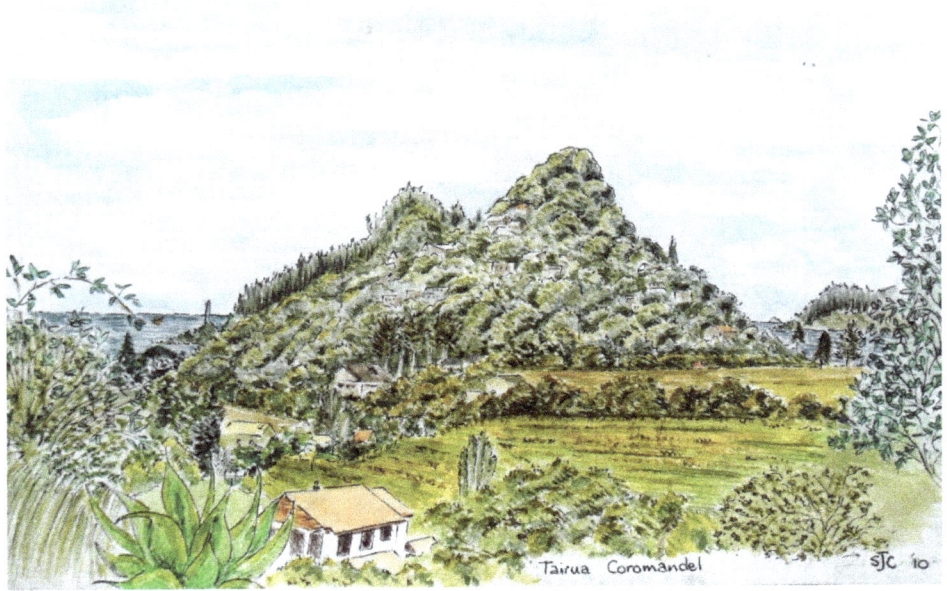

Another great spot to sit and watch the world go by is to the side of the Ferry Building down at the harbour front. This is part of the modernised Ferry terminal for Devonport and Waiheke and on occasions the huge cruise liners dock nearby next to the Hilton Hotel. The Ferry Building was built in 1912 on reclaimed land and is of sandstone and brick construction. The base is Coromandel granite.

There was initial objection to the building, as it would obstruct harbour views. It underwent a comprehensive restoration in 1986. Its architecture is based on the Edwardian Baroque style. The ferries and the building itself lost some of their popularity when the harbour bridge was opened in 1959 but following the 1986 restoration and adjacent developments at Britomart rail and major bus interchange, business has flourished.

My sketch portrays just part of the ornate architecture of the west side of the building.

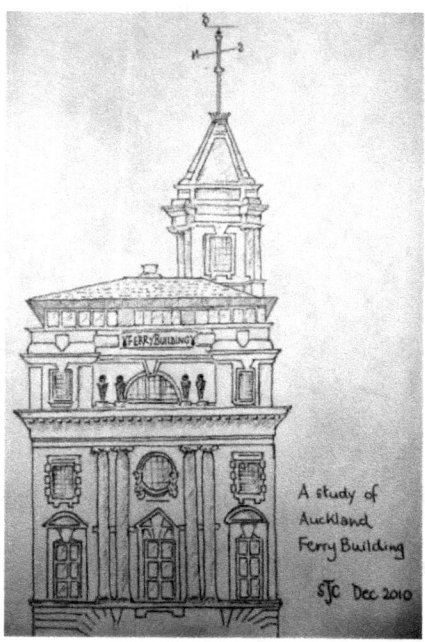

The following is a view from a bach that we rented for New Year 2010/11. You can see the sandspit of dunes that forms a protected channel of water which connects the Heads and village with the peripheral areas. There is a strong local Māori history. The hapū (clan or descent group) of Te Uri-o-Hau, which descended from the iwi (tribe) of Ngāti Whātua has become the iwi of Kaipara. The name Mangawhai is probably derived from 'Manga' meaning stream or river and 'Whai' from Te Whai who was a chief who fled from the Ngāpuhi tribe and settled on the headland where the river meets.

European settlers purchased land in this area in the 19th century. There has been much historical confusion as to the legal status of these Crown and second wave purchases (see the comprehensive analysis by Barry Rigby, 'The Crown, Māori and Mahurangi', 1998). Settlers subsequently transformed the bush into farmland and collected Kauri gum and timber.

Over the last 50 years the area has become a popular area for holiday visitors, boatees, art and Bennet's Chocolate factory!

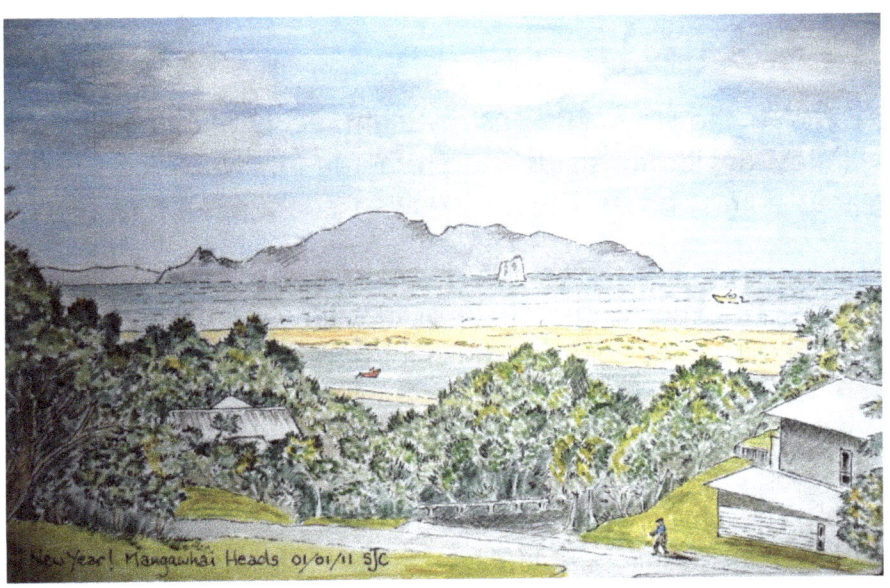

I went to the Devonport Food and Wine festival in 2011 and enjoyed sampling the various wines, food and listening to the live music. I was looking for a 'stable' group to sketch and was a bit embarrassed to be concentrating on individuals so, after some preliminary outlines, I took a photo of the revellers and completed the sketch at home.

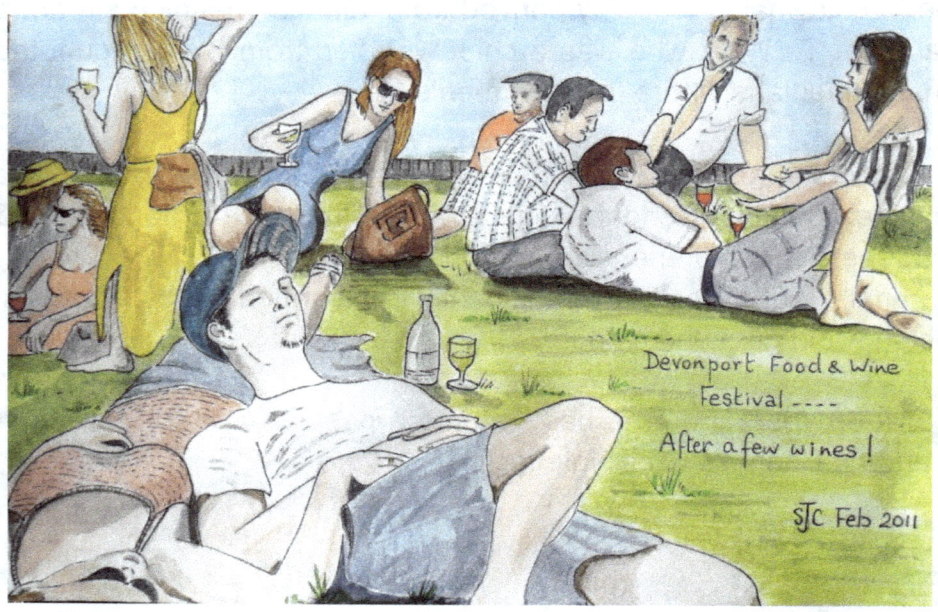

I needed to return to the UK in 2012 as my mum had been admitted to hospital in Winchester. I stayed with my sister and brother-in-law who also live there. Mum died during that admission and there followed some weeks of sorting out her estate.

As a way of easing some of the stress of that time I took my sketchbook and chose this scene with a city gate to the right and the adjacent Pilgrim School's Headmaster's house. The school was established at this site in 1931 and became a 'preparatory school for choristers and non-choristers alike, with the purpose of allowing each to benefit from the many talents of the other', according to their website. The building was redesigned in the 17th century and, like many other historic buildings in this beautiful city, it sits on former Roman and medieval sites.

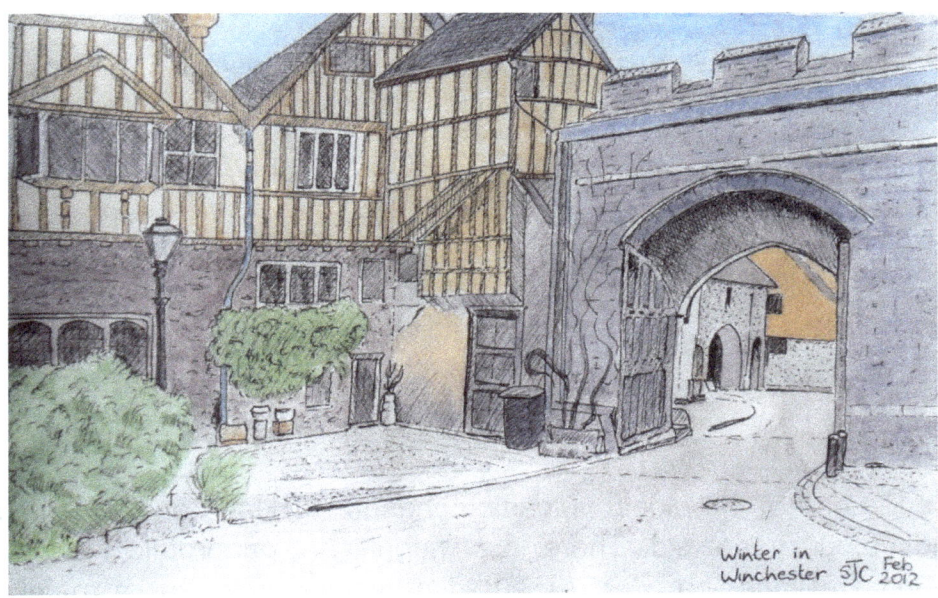

During a subsequent trip back to the Midlands in the UK, I visited the village Ironbridge and managed to find a great spot to view the famous Iron Bridge from a bank across the river Severn, which runs through the village. This was the first arch bridge (designed by Thomas Pritchard and built by Abraham Darby) in the world to be constructed of cast iron. Local iron ore was smelted with coke in the early 18th century and in view of the favourable price and availability of local fuel, Shropshire became a centre of cast iron production.

As the river Severn was a significant trading route, the bridge needed to be high enough to allow tall ships to pass. Construction took 4 years and used 378 tons of iron. It was opened in 1781. The bridge survived the great flood of 1795 due to its considerable strength.

In 1997 a small watercolour sketch was discovered and this revealed details of how the bridge had been built with a wooden framework which was used to raise the half-ribs from the deck of a vessel.

In 1934 it was closed to vehicles and pedestrians were charged a toll to pass across the bridge up until 1950.

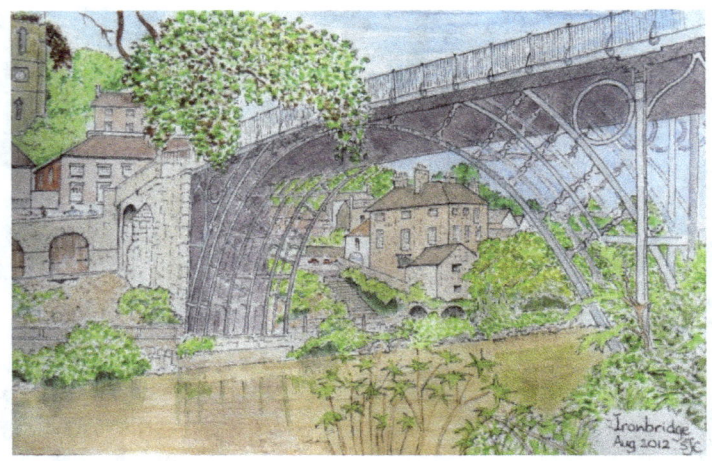

North Head is one of the oldest volcanic cones in Auckland and is estimated to be around 50,000 years old. There is a magnificent panoramic view over the Hauraki Gulf and inner harbour. As noted previously, this was a major site of coastal defences. Kids would enjoy sitting on cardboard and sliding down the grassy slopes. Looking up towards North Shore the first beach in view is Cheltenham Beach and the following is a sketch from that site looking out to the Rangitoto volcano across the channel. This is the entry channel for all the container ships and cruisers and also a good spot to catch Snapper provided you watch out for the incoming ships!

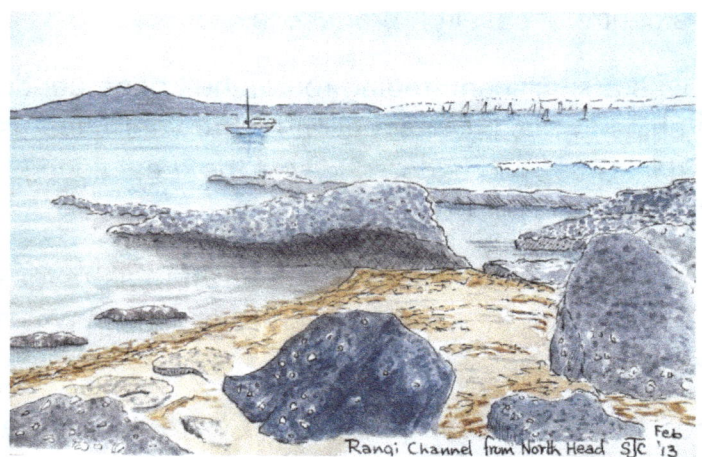

To the east of the city centre along Tamaki Drive lies Mission Bay. It takes its name from the Melanesian Mission which was established there at the end of the 1840s. The stone buildings close to the beach date from 1858 and were built from scoria rock which was quarried on Rangitoto. The fountain forms a centre piece for the Mission Bay Reserve. It is constructed of Sicilian marble and has three bronze sea monsters from which jets of water gush. It is also used as a paddling pool in the summer and the reserve is a popular venue for jazz and blues festivals, family beach gatherings and arts and crafts markets. It is a very popular venue for families to gather and beach party over the Christmas holiday.

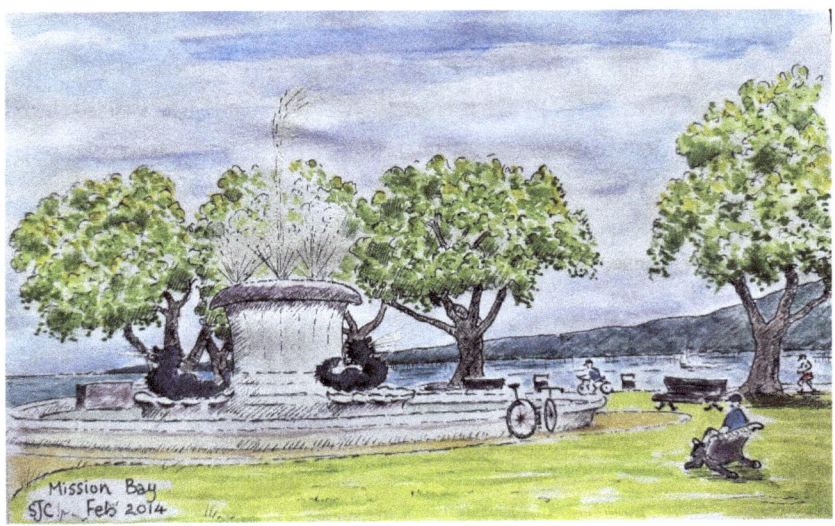

I joined the Plein Air Painters of New Zealand Meet Up group in 2014 which was excellently organised by the artist Jennifer Cruden and many of my subsequent sketches were done while out with this group. The following was on one such outing to Alberton House, on the day it celebrated its 150th anniversary. This colonial mansion, with suggestions of Indian architectural influence, such as decorative verandas and towers, was built in 1863 and was owned by a leading socialite family, the Kerr Taylors, in Mount Albert. The house was subsequently left to Heritage New Zealand in 1972.

In the foreground of the sketch you can see one of our plein air members, painting in oils.

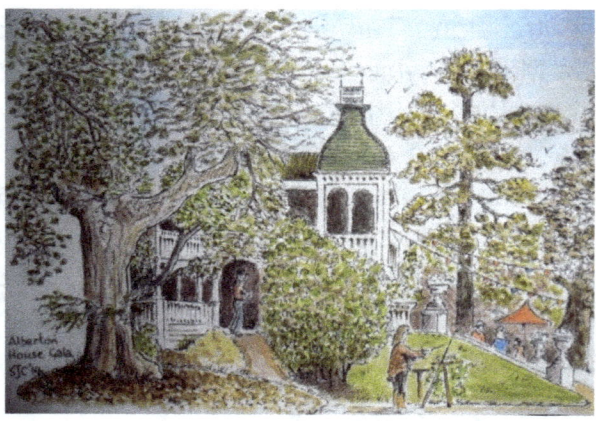

There are some lovely views from the marina at Westhaven out to the Auckland CBD and the next view was one of those which was nicely bordered by trees and foliage. The Sky Tower dominates much of the landscape in this area and there are magnificent panoramic views from its upper decks.

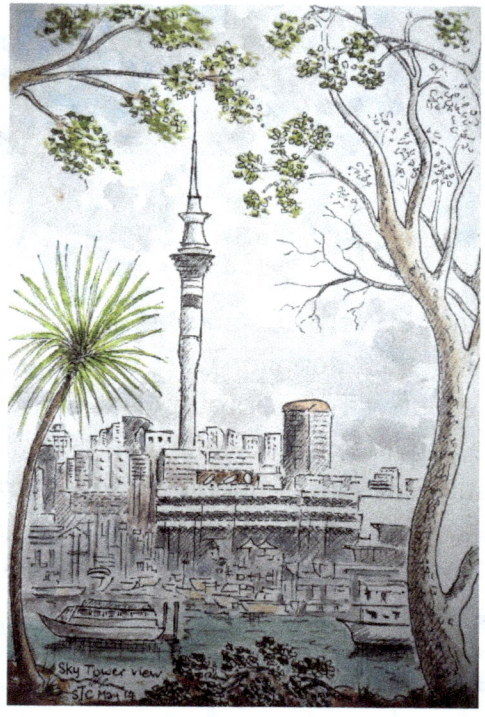

The tower took two years and nine months to construct and was opened in 1997. It is designed to withstand an 8.0 magnitude earthquake within a 20 mile radius, winds in excess of 200 km/hr and can sway up to one metre in such winds! It is 328 metres high and, apart from its three observation decks, has a revolving restaurant and a 'Sky jump' controlled by a guide cable. It is also used for telecommunications and broadcasting.

Another favourite place to visit and sketch is the Howick Historical Village. It serves as a 'living history museum' reflecting Auckland's colonial period between 1840 - 1880. The local iwi of that area were the Ngāi Tai people of Tainui descent and had lived there for around 300 years.

The missionary, William Fairburn, bought 40,000 acres of land from Māori with his life savings and in 1840 the government took 36,000 acres for use as 'Fencible' settlements and sold most of the remaining land to settlers. Retired soldiers were given land with the understanding that they would act as defence forces should the need arise.

The word 'Fencible' comes from the word 'defensible'. They were to serve for seven years in exchange for a cottage and an acre of land. Māori recognised the advantage of such cooperation and trade and Māori labourers built the settlers cottages under Royal Engineers supervision. A total of 721 men along with their families comprised a final total of 2,500 new settlers (many were from Ireland and had served in the British army at the time of the famine).

The subject of this next sketch at the Historical Village is a 'settler's cottage' which was built for settlers as semi-permanent accommodation on Fencible farm allotments. The walls were turf block and the roof constructed from Kahikatea rafters and Nīkau palm fronds. Wood and glass windows were added in some cases. The chimney was built from wood which was lined with sod for fire protection. These cottages were also known colloquially as 'sod cottages' or 'soddies'.

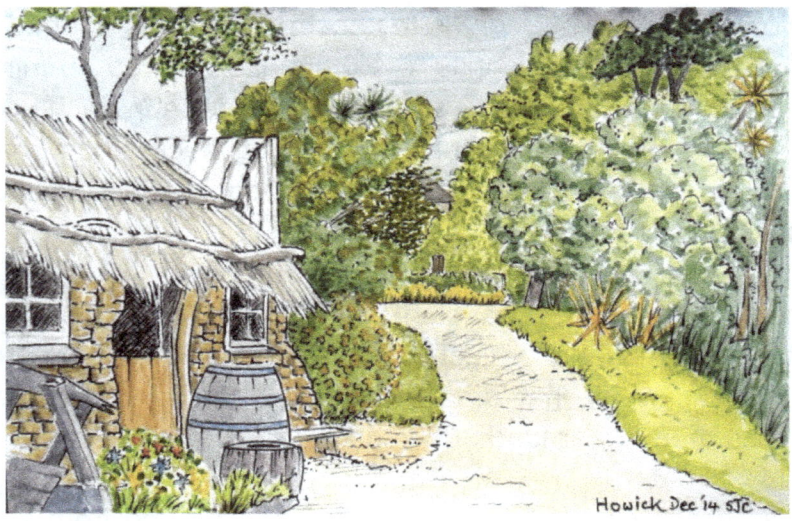

The following is an oil painting of the same 'settler's cottage' looking across the lake from the other side.

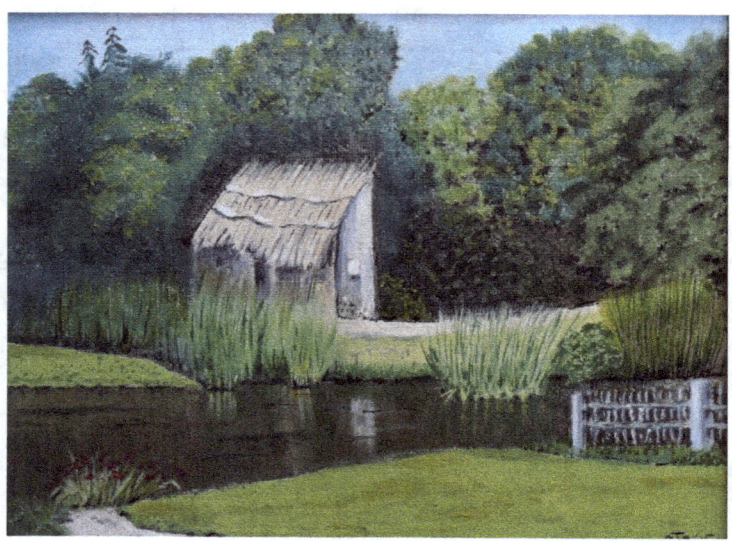

The Plein Air Group occasionally takes trips to picturesque areas and stays for a couple of days. One such trip was out to Manukau Heads and included stays at Big Bay and Matakawau.

The sketch at Big Bay was plein air but relies a lot on artistic license as it was bucketing down at the time. I completed it from the shelter of the bach veranda and turned it in to a beautiful dawn!

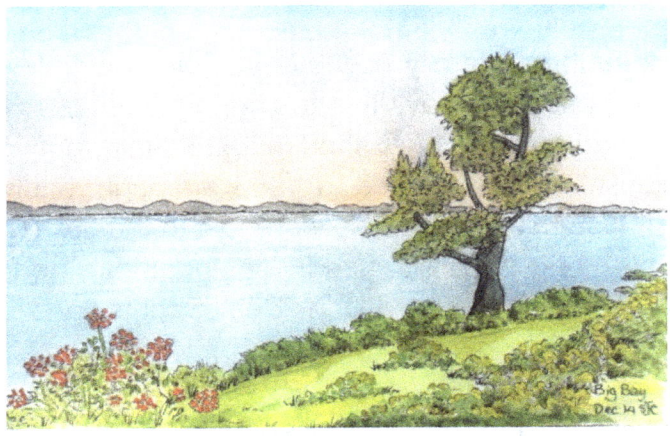

The bach at Matakawau overlooks a lovely beach and the Pōhutakawa trees were just breaking out in blossom as we were there in early December.

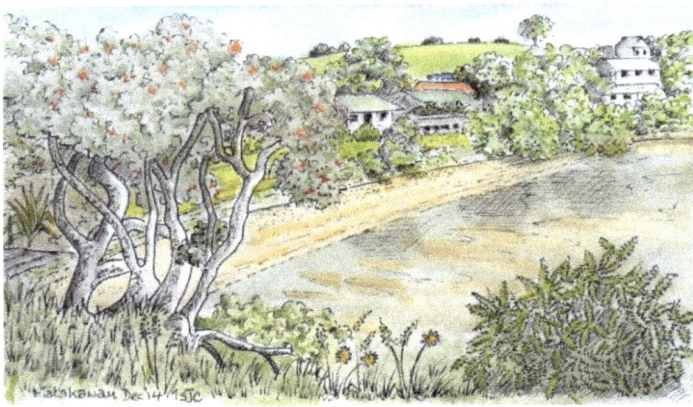

One of New Zealand's worst maritime disasters was just off-shore when HMS Orpheus ran aground on the Manukau Bar in 1863 and sank with the loss of 189 lives. This sand bar remains dangerous. Manukau lighthouse and signal station overlook the Manukau bar and looking north across the harbour are the Waitākere ranges. Looking directly down the 240 metres from the lighthouse, one of the world's rarest and endangered dolphins (Māui) can be seen. We were lucky that Jennifer, our organiser, knows the lighthouse keepers and this gave us a privileged visit and guided tour.

Both my son's and daughter's family now live in Point Chevalier and my trip to their homes takes me past Coxs bay. The following sketch is of the Hawke Sea Scouts Hall which started out as a boat shed in 1928. A fire gutted the building in 1952 and the new building was opened in 1953 although, sadly, a lot of gear, trophies and items of historical importance were lost in the fire. The hall is known locally as 'The Ship' and is also used for theatrical performances. Our granddaughters have recently joined the Sea Scouts and are loving the experience.

The potential, from this site, for some awe-inspiring sunsets is great and equally when the moon is full and the tide is high there are some lovely water reflections across the bay.

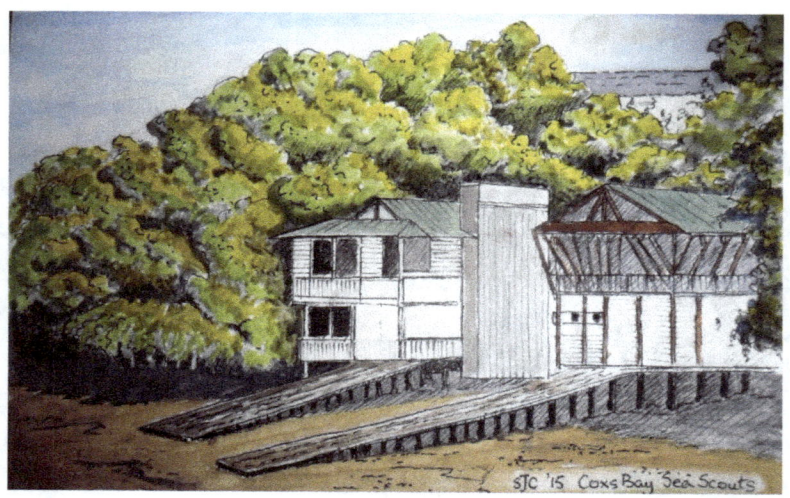

The developments at the Wynyard Quarter comprise a large variety of quality restaurants, viaduct events centre, the fish market, dock line tramway, Silo 6 art and exhibition space, sea plane base and waterfront walks. The whole area has been developed as part of the preparations for the America's Cup and to put the 'cherry on the cake' New Zealand have now retained the cup in 2021.

On a day out with the Plein Air Group I sketched the viaduct events centre and one of the fishing vessels tied up alongside that day. You can see one of our members who is also painting the boat close up!

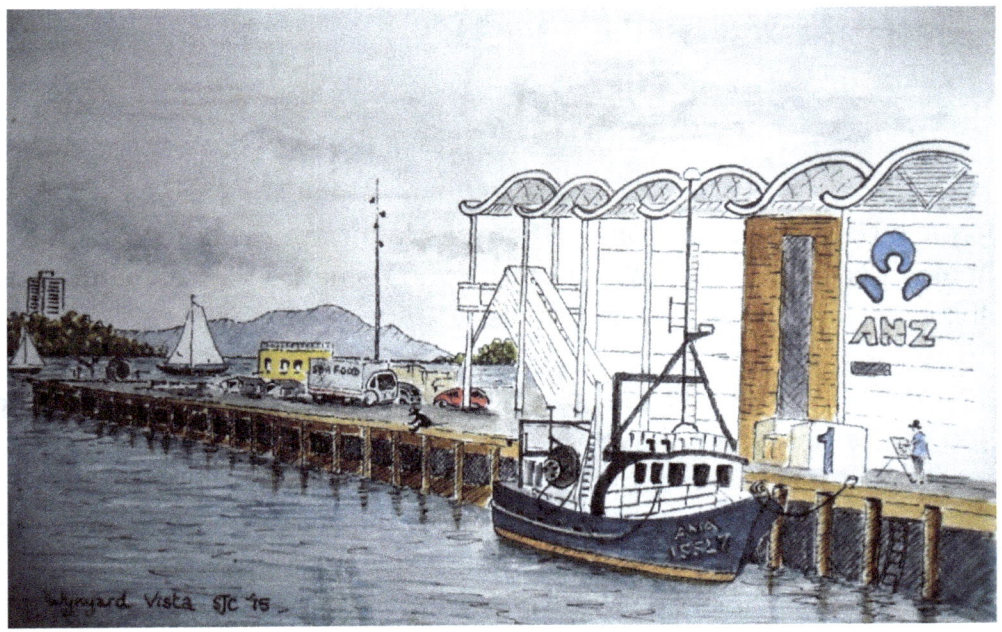

Back to Howick Historical Village, which is a great source of sketching material.

The following sketch is of John Bycroft's flour mill and in the background, on the left, is a reproduction of a charcoal burners camp.

I'm afraid my ability to draw a circle (the mill wheel) free hand was clearly challenged in this sketch!

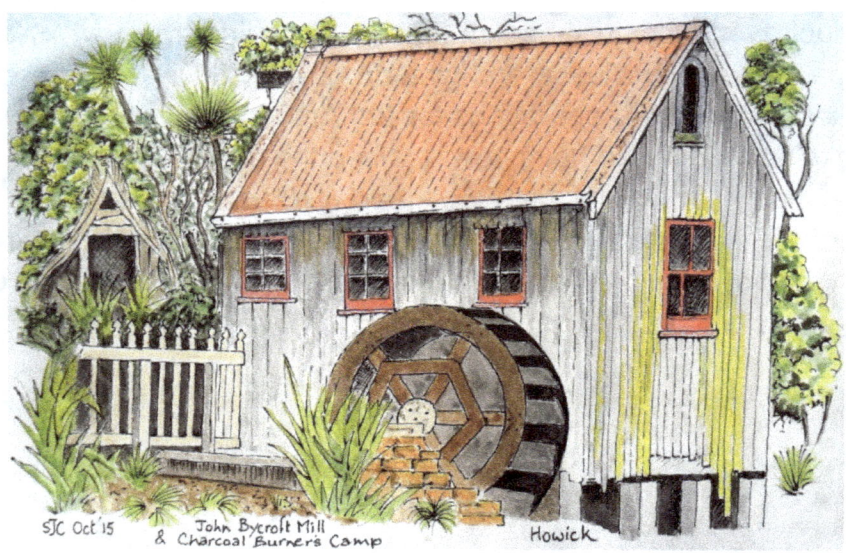

John Bycroft Mill & Charcoal Burners Camp, Howick

John Bycroft built the original mill in 1855 at Manurewa. The iron work of the water wheel is from the original but the mill stone came from his Onehunga flour mill and this was powered by water from the Onehunga springs.

Charcoal burning is a craft that goes back centuries. Charcoal burners working in camps led a rather lonely life, having to live near the kiln in basic accommodation. It was an important industry, especially at Whitford where the alternatives of farming were defeated by the poor quality clay soils. The charcoal was sold as fuel for domestic use and industrial use in brickmaking, blacksmithing and tinsmithing. The New Zealand camps followed the traditional British format.

Alan La Roche was the honorary director of Howick Historical village and his research into this particular subject provides personal history of individuals who worked in this trade. He records George Hamilton, a bachelor, who lived in the bush in a 'wretched cabin'. He would cut and burn ti tree. Having need of a wife, he went to Auckland and bought one for 10 pounds! They lived a miserable existence, exposed to the dirt, hard work, carbon monoxide fumes, potential burns and all for poor returns.

This was the last sketch in my first book, some 8 years since I started, and after this I tended to concentrate on producing oil paintings; a medium I have grown to love. This involved trips out to various picturesque venues around the greater Auckland area to meet with fellow plein air artists with all the gear that oil painting requires; a pochade box, paints, thinner, solvent, rags, easel, brushes, fold up seat and drying box to keep paintings from touching anything while still drying. However, after receiving a gift of a new sketch book from my daughter, I was stimulated to start sketching again in 2016.

The following sketch is of Western Springs which is close to where my daughter's family live. They will often visit this very picturesque venue and the girls love to see all the birdlife that live on the lake in this large park. This includes black swans, pukeko, coots, mallard ducks, geese, gulls and shags. Large eels congregate around the edges of the lake and carp can be seen mingling with them.

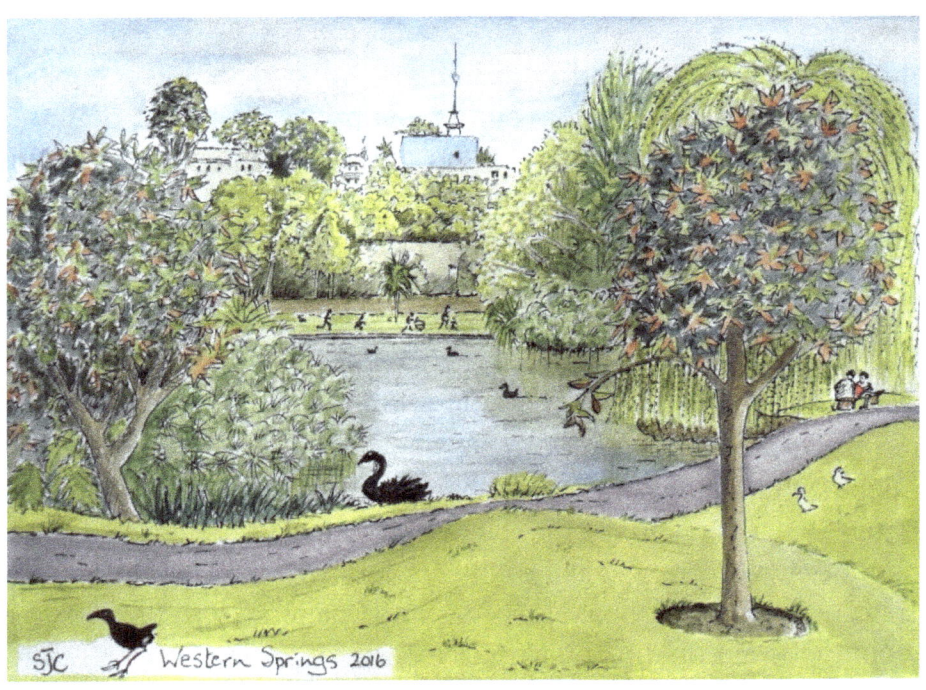

Western Springs (Waiōrea) was valued by Māori for the fresh, clear spring waters and the eels that lived (and still do) in the feeder stream. After colonisation, a Scottish settler, William Motion, farmed the land around the springs. In 1874 the city bought his mill and land including the spring and in 1875 the surrounding swampy area was converted into a 15 acre artificial lake. This involved removing 20,000 cartloads of spoil from the site!

A pump house pumped water to new reservoirs but ultimately this didn't provide enough for the city and new reservoirs made the springs redundant. The area deteriorated over time and became a boggy area full of dumped rubbish, mosquitoes and rats. In 1961 the Council reclaimed the lake which had become choked with waterweed and all the rubbish was cleared away. By the 1980s, following major landscaping, it was transformed into a very attractive park, lake, islands and wetlands. The adjacent Museum of Transport and Technology (MOTAT) and Zoo compliment the whole area. Some of the world's most famous musical acts have performed at Western Springs stadium.

No Auckland sketchbook would be complete without some recognition of The Domain, considering it is its largest and oldest park. It is based on the rim of the Pukekawa volcano which erupted around 150,000 years ago. The museum is built on the rim remnant of the volcano. Construction was completed in 1929 and it is considered to be one of the finest Greco-Roman buildings in the Southern Hemisphere. There have been a number of renovations and additions since then.

The Domain duck ponds are fresh water springs which are derived from the ground water that drains what was the crater lake and swamp. Māori settlement in this area comprised gardens and some terracing of hill slopes. This was ideal for habitation, with the flat swampy remains of the crater providing plenty of water and eels but Pukekawa actually means 'hill of bitter memories' recalling the tribal battles fought between Hongi Hika of the Ngāpuhi from the north and Pōtatau Te Wherowhero who lead the local Ngāti Whātua. Ultimately Pukekawa was part of the land sold to the Europeans by Ngāti Whātua.

By 1860 the swampy land had been drained and cricket fields established there. The Domain duck ponds are a lovely spot to sit and sketch with plenty of shade and lots of wildfowl activity. Apart from the flora it was possible to learn quite a bit about various duck postures over the couple of hours spent there! This is one of the spin offs of plein air painting. There is a lot going on around you while you spend maybe 3 to 4 hours in one spot (apart for an occasional nip to the loo). This can vary from animal to human behaviour, water sports (I never cease to wonder at the variety of ways human beings can interact with the surface of the water) and of course the interaction with the general public.

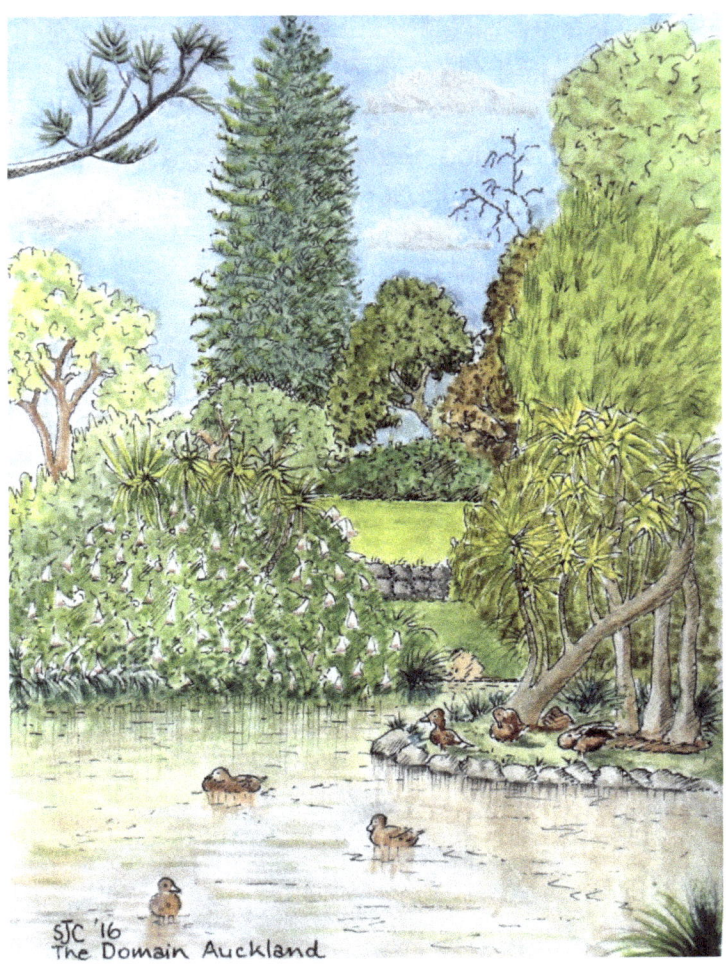

This may involve being surrounded by a coach load of tourists, children commenting on your efforts with no inhibitions, various bugs committing suicide in your newly applied oil paint, one to one chats with enthusiastic passers-by and magic moments when a bird perches transiently on the top of your easel or when the sky and its reflection changes through a whole palette of colours as the sun starts to settle.

The next sketch will always be printed in my memory as I got a call from son Mike in the middle of this visit to the Viaduct harbour area announcing the birth of our first grandson, Finn. Mareesa had achieved this all in the space of 4 hours. Probably about the length of time I spent on this sketch! However, the masterpiece that they created far outweighed my day's efforts! City scapes are all well and good but being of a somewhat obsessional nature I'm afraid such sketches are a bit of a challenge too far and it is a bit like putting together a jigsaw – rather frustrating interlocking the various sections but ultimately satisfying if they fit together comfortably.

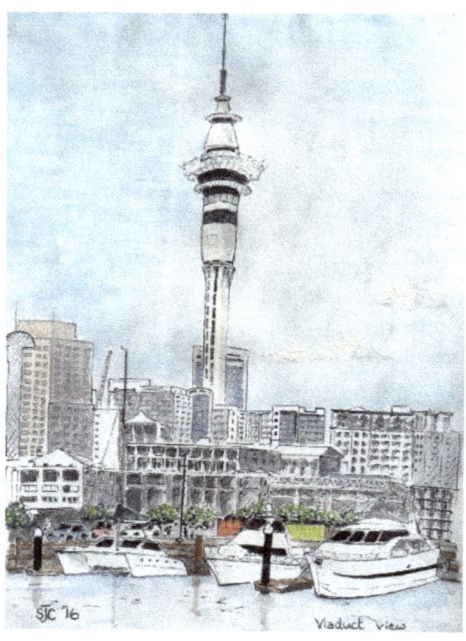

As I mentioned earlier, visiting picturesque sites with the Plein Air Group has stimulated me to try alternative media and I now enjoy mixing my sketches with oil paintings. However, I still need to relax a bit with larger canvases, brushes and chunks of paint! My tendency to put in too much detail is a follow on from the years of sketching. The following is a typical example of one of my 7 x 9 inch oil paintings of Western Springs on canvas board. Perhaps one day I will get out into the mountains with a large canvas, large paint brushes and let go!

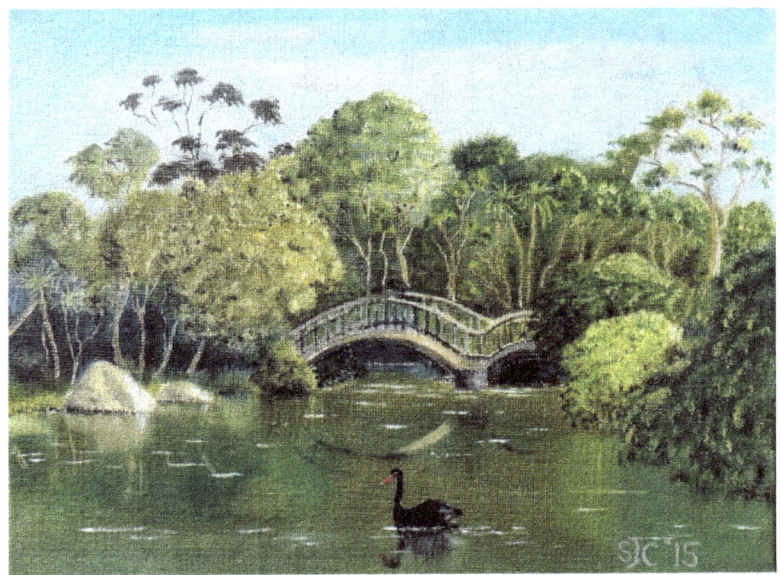

I've thoroughly enjoyed putting this collection together. Each sketch reminds me of a moment in time rather like music from the past takes you back to an earlier part of life.

I've learnt a lot more about the history attached to many of these lovely views and it has given me a greater appreciation of the evolution of this beautiful country that is now our home. This was how far I got in the first edition and as 3 years had passed I thought I would continue with an update. From a selfish point of view, it acts as a kind of picture diary but if anyone else is interested then I will always love to share my experiences.

An Update

One of the favourite sites to visit with members of Plein Air Painters NZ is the Waiake bay in Torbay. The following sketch shows one of the members painting the view of the Tor. He is accompanied by his wife. What a great way to relax and enjoy the scenery.

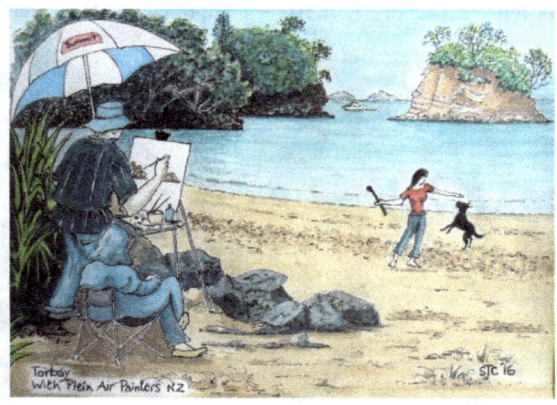

The Tor has featured in a number of my paintings and this one is oil on canvas and is the only copy I have (the original was given away). There is some abnormal colouring to the right – probably due to some faulty camera technique.

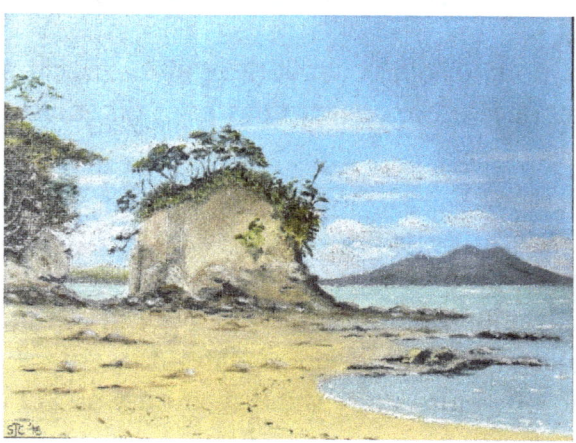

Around the corner there is a lovely little bay called Winstone's Cove which provides a view of the Tor from the other side. An interesting historical footnote to this site is that the names of the tracks leading from the cove are 'Moonshine Run' and 'Revenue Run' reflecting the occupations of some early settlers who were into illegal wine making and moonshining! The following is a watercolour from this spot.

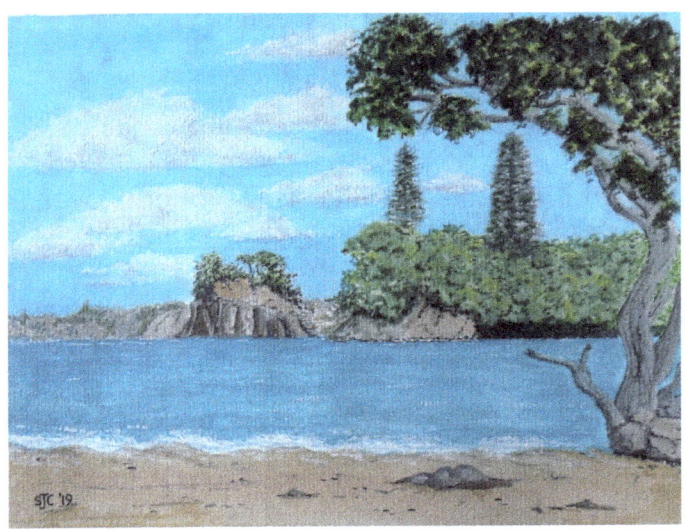

Just below Tor Bay is Brown's bay. It is named after the Brown family who moved there in 1876 having purchased 136 acres. It was transformed into a working farm and by the 1900s it was a popular destination for holiday makers travelling by steamer.

The sandstone cliffs were originally formed under the sea and gradually rose up with layers of soft mudstone and siltstone formed millions of years ago.

Having chosen my spot alongside the cliff face I was interrupted by a young lad who informed me that there was a significant risk of falling rocks where I was sitting. Some time after that visit there was a news item about someone being injured at that same spot!

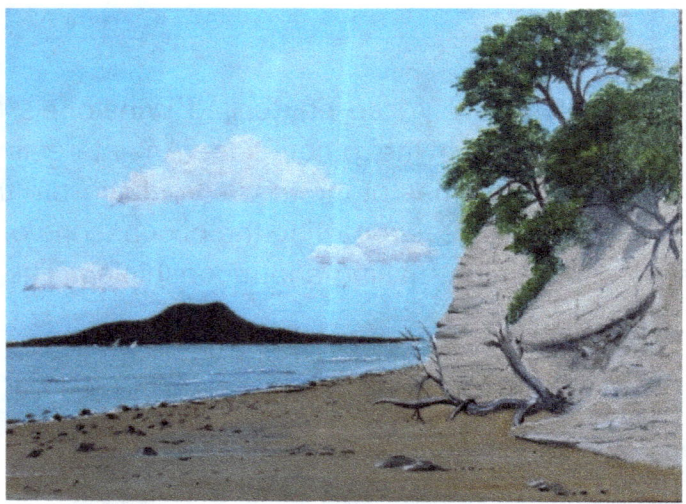

I've spent quite a bit of time painting in Devonport over the years and the following are some examples of local scenery.

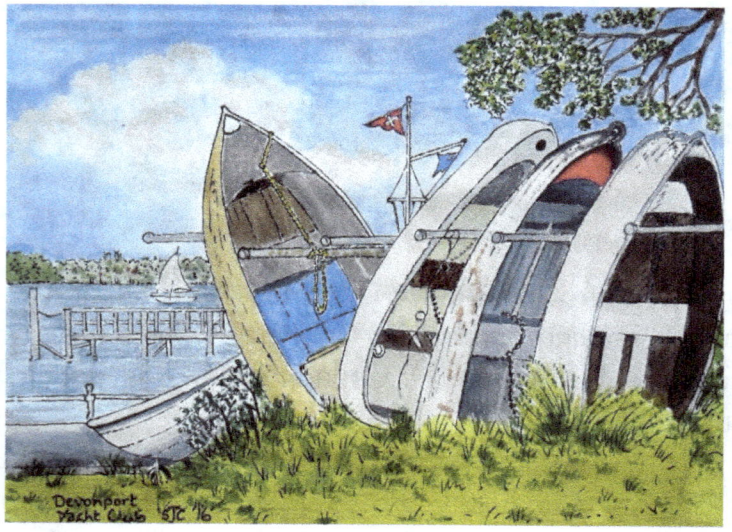

These boats were all chained up at the yacht club and made an interesting group subject. They are certainly in use as I have revisited a number of times and there have been variations in the ensemble!

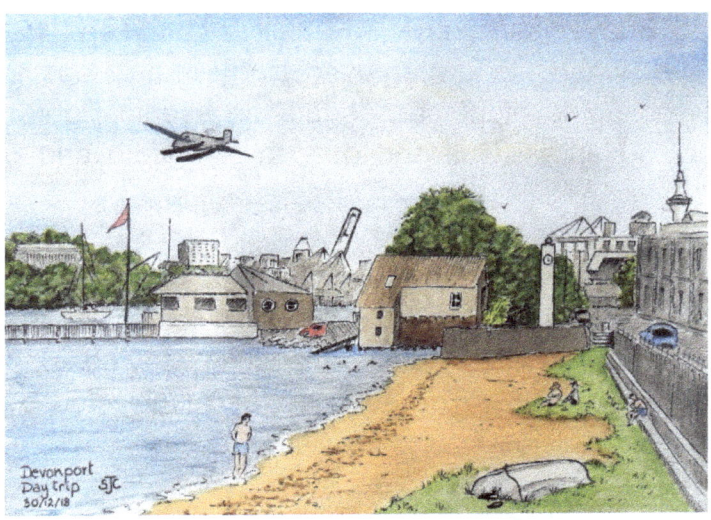

I had to keep a rough idea in my mind of the shape and perspective of the sea plane as it flew over while sketching this view which looks beyond the yacht club towards the ferry terminal. On a separate trip I got a much closer view of the plane as it did its circuit around Auckland harbour but captured the detail later from a photo I took at the time. I couldn't get the plane to stop long enough for me to sketch it!

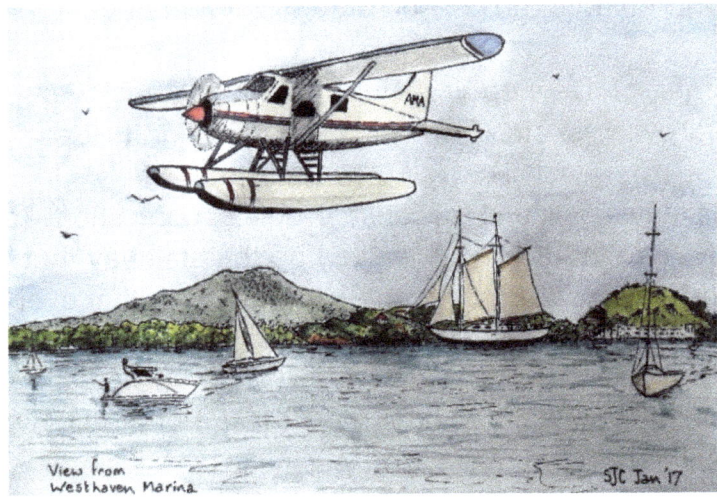

This de Havilland Beaver sea plane was built in 1961 and was previously flying in Vancouver where its owner used to fly short hops to his fishing lodge. It now takes up to eight passengers on scenic flights all over the Waitematā harbour, Hauraki Gulf and over to Rangitoto and Great Barrier island.

It is based in the Wynyard Quarter, although it has been shifted about since the America's Cup developments. It can be seen taking off in just 400m of water. Auckland has a long history of sea plane flights which operated on the Waitematā Harbour until 1989. The service was resurrected by the current company in 2013.

Sea planes were considered to be the height of glamorous travel in Aotearoa's past. Seventy-five years ago, a flying boat named Aotearoa flew from Auckland to Sydney and pioneered international air travel in the South Pacific.

Two retired sea planes, the Sunderland and the Aranui flying boats are now restored and can be seen in the MOTAT museum. The latter serviced the Tasman Empire Airways Ltd (TEAL), flying between Auckland, Suva, Aitutaki, Tahiti and Apia, which ceased around 50 years ago.

Around the corner of Devonport's North Head is the lovely Cheltenham Beach and the following sketch is the view towards North Head.

I remember this day's painting because I got 'caught short' (probably too much coffee) and needed the loo. I walked up the stairway that you can see in the picture and kept heading up North Head expecting at every turn to find a public loo.

Unfortunately it wasn't until I reached the top that I found one, by which time I was bursting! If you look carefully you can just see a distant figure that I added looking out over the channel, standing on a prominent ramp, because that's where I stood after I had relieved myself!

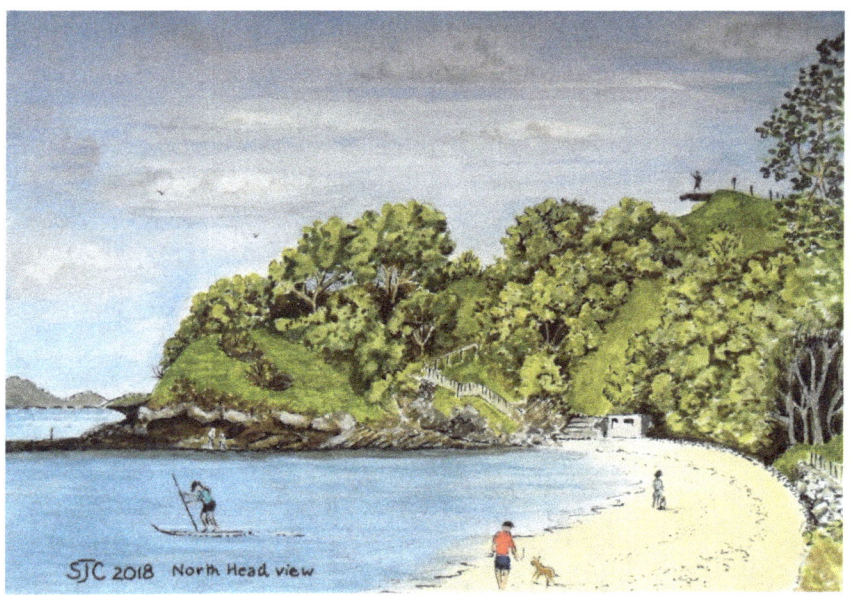

The following is an oil painting from the same area looking out to Rangitoto.

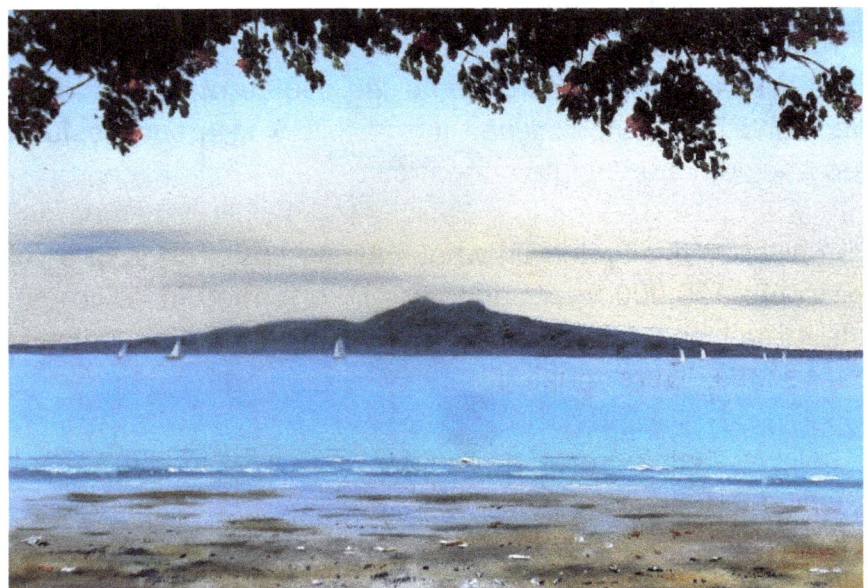

Further up North Shore we come to Takapuna and the following is the view from the end of the jetty at the PumpHouse, situated in Killarney Park on the shore of Lake Pupuke.

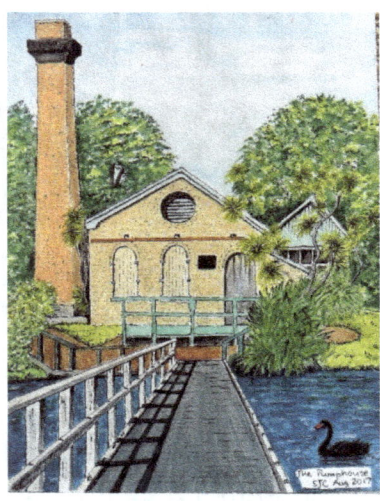

It was originally built in 1905 and was a water pumping station that pumped water from the lake to the early settlers of Devonport. It fell into disrepair when the Waitakere Ranges became the source of Auckland's water. Local art lovers and historians rescued it and following a successful fund raising, restored and converted it into a theatre.

The PumpHouse is situated on what was the crater edge of a volcano which erupted some 150,000 years ago. The lake formed in its crater and is 57m deep. It is Auckland's only volcanic crater lake. This lends itself to a perfect venue for scuba divers' training.

Some believe that there is a 'ghostly presence' in the PumpHouse, with some feeling that they are being watched, flashes of someone watching from Stage Right and missing props that reappear without explanation. A psychic medium has identified this 'presence' as Peg Escott who was a founding member of the trust board that saved the PumpHouse.

Back in 2009 I sketched the Old Post Office at Three Lamps in Ponsonby. Now in its next stage of life it is a restaurant called Augustus (presumably after the poor post master who was murdered). The following is a different view of the building and this time with a watercolour wash.

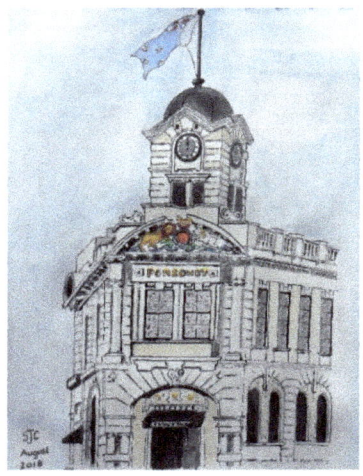

I also sketched the Ferry building in 2010, but just with black pen. So here is my follow up plein air pen and wash, sitting on the same bench as last time.

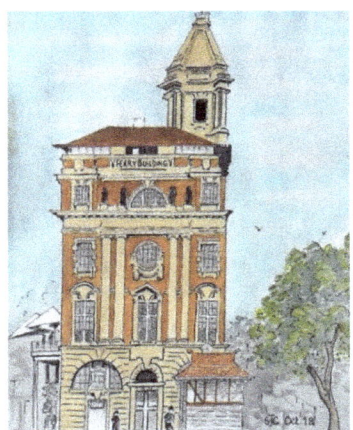

Although I have travelled to sites all around the Auckland area, there are plenty of views quite close to home. This one is an oil painting of Coxs Bay which is 2 minutes' drive away and I was sitting in the shade to the far right of the Sea Scouts' Hall. The weather and the tide were changing rapidly that day.

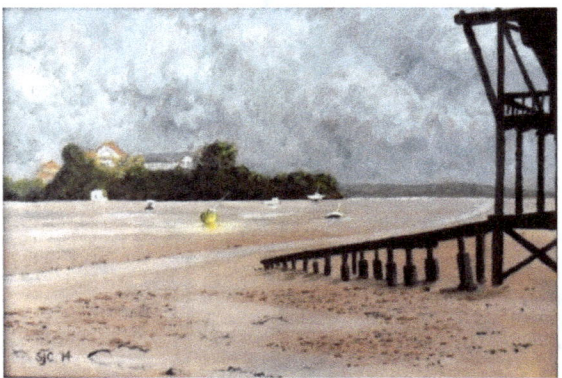

A favourite walk is from Herne Bay down to Westhaven, past all the expectant fishermen who set themselves up along the strip before the harbour bridge. This is the view out to Watchman Island that they would see while waiting for the big catch that never seems to come.

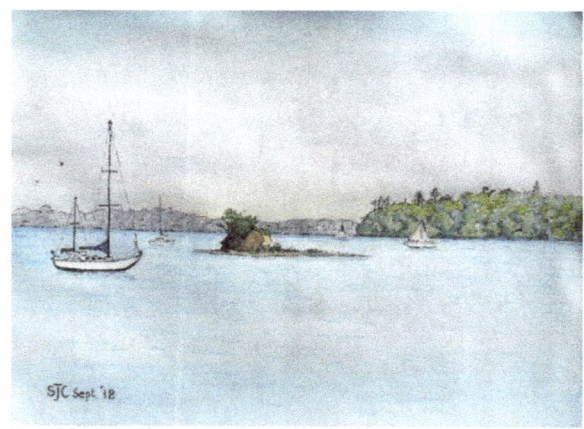

Watchman Island has an interesting history, in that it has an undefined legal status. It is the small sandstone island in the middle of the picture above. It was known as Sentinel Rock in the mid-19th century and it is gradually being worn away. However, in 2011 a Māori Sovereignty flag was raised on the island but this has subsequently been removed. Some local iwi are considered to have customary rights over it. It is occasionally visited by kayakers and dinghy sailors.

Just a few more steps to the roundabout by Ponsonby Cruise Club and there we find a very agreeable 'watering hole' previously called the Sitting Duck Café. Out on the deck there is a great view of Westhaven and all the resident boats. A great place to stop for a 'Flat White' and a read of the papers.

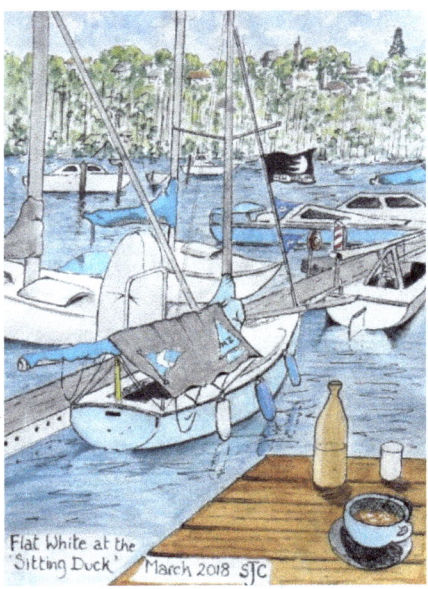

After the reviving coffee it's just another step to the boardwalk that will take us to the Wynyard Quarter and Viaduct area. Since its opening in 2005 this popular promenade takes us along the water's edge.

The timber is Spotted Gum hardwood and will survive for years in this marine environment. A summer's weekend will guarantee a mix of walkers, joggers, cyclists and scooters (including the latest introduction of electric scooters to Auckland!). This is the view from Westhaven beach at St Mary's bay.

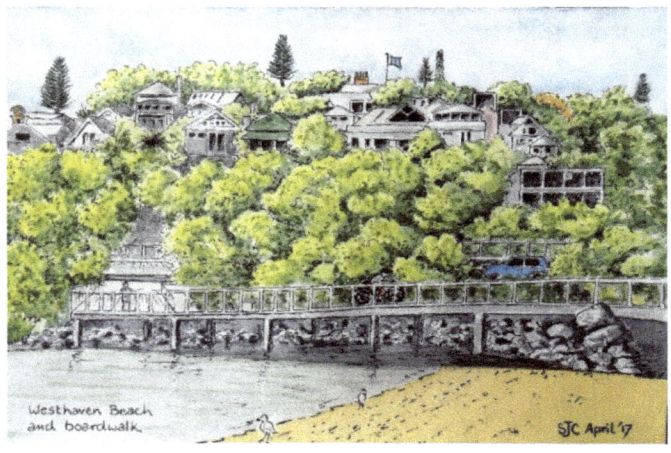

During a break in Whangamata, I spent the afternoon watching all the antics on the harbour wharf at the mouth of the Wentworth river.

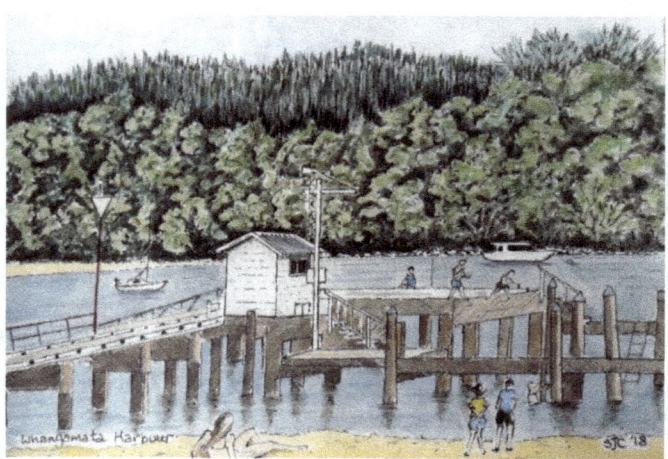

These two seemed to be watching me sketch while resting at the Whangamata estuary and made excellent subjects.

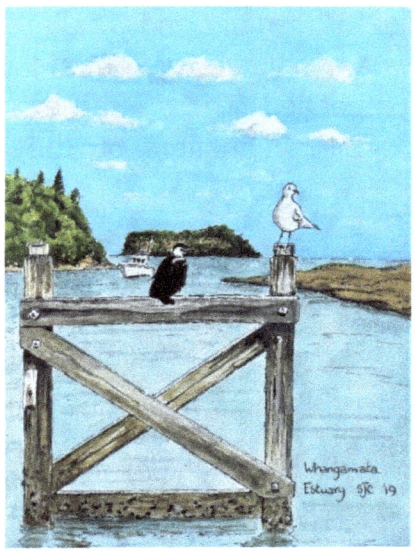

And this view from Whangamata beach was a bit of a trial as I started to get bitten by some ants while sitting in the dunes! I used a white gel pen to enhance the breaking waves.

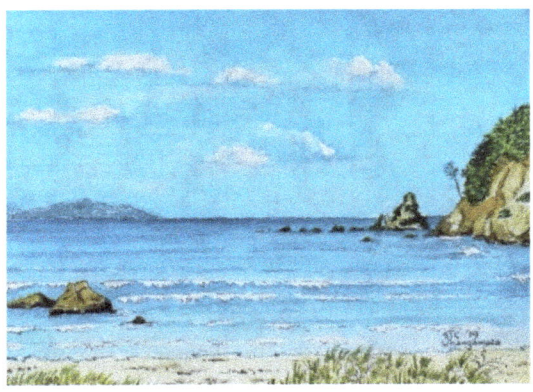

I haven't done that much proper urban sketching having tended to concentrate on land and seascapes but I have recently discovered some lovely scenes tucked away in Albert Park in central Auckland city. It was a military barracks in the mid-19th century and was built on the previous site of Te Horotiu pā. The park was eventually laid out in the 1880s and the design was based on a public competition. There is an extensive series of tunnels underneath, built in 1941 for air raid shelters, but they are all sealed up now.

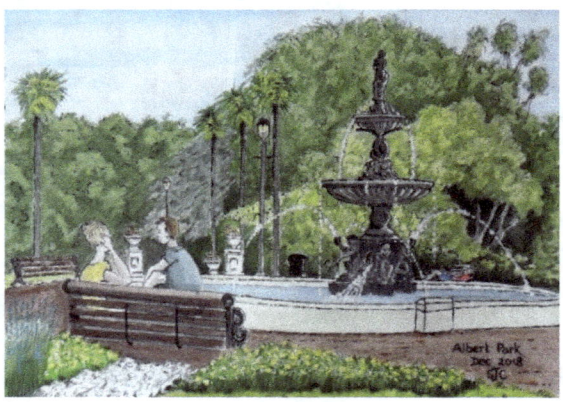

And a further park setting.

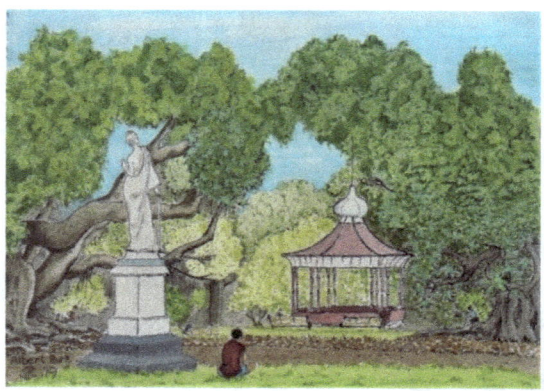

There are some scenes that I am keen to revisit but usually to try an alternative medium. This is the view of Western Springs that I included at an earlier stage of the book. On this occasion I reverted from oil to pen and wash and enjoyed mixing a wide variety of greens which are fully represented in the surrounding foliage.

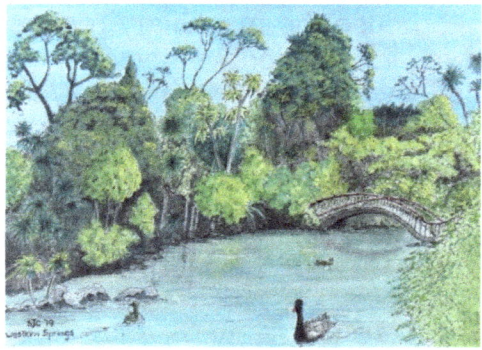

Walking down the Wynyard quarter I would often see this puppeteer who would gyrate his skeleton puppet to Elvis and other rock numbers with great effect. The children passing by would be totally captivated by the show. He gave me permission to sketch him.

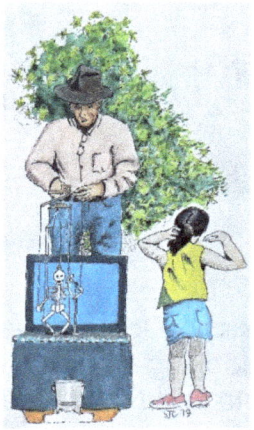

Our grandchildren love to visit MOTAT (Museum of Transport and Technology). In 1960 the Old Time Transport Preservation League, the Royal Aeronautical Society (New Zealand) and the Historic Auckland Society joined together and established MOTAT at Western Springs. In 1963 the land was transferred to MOTAT and the Museum opened to the public in 1964 on its current site, Te Wai Ōrea which in Māori means 'waters of the eel'.

The site includes a brick pumping house which is preserved as Category 2 Historic Place. It was built to house the machinery required to pump water from the lake to the reservoirs in Ponsonby between 1877–1910. This was subsequently supplemented by water supply from the Waitākere Ranges.

Next to this stands a McLaren steam traction engine which was built in the UK in about 1912 and was a working engine in the Christchurch area for many years. Many of these engines were either used in pairs to pull ploughs or drive threshing machines.

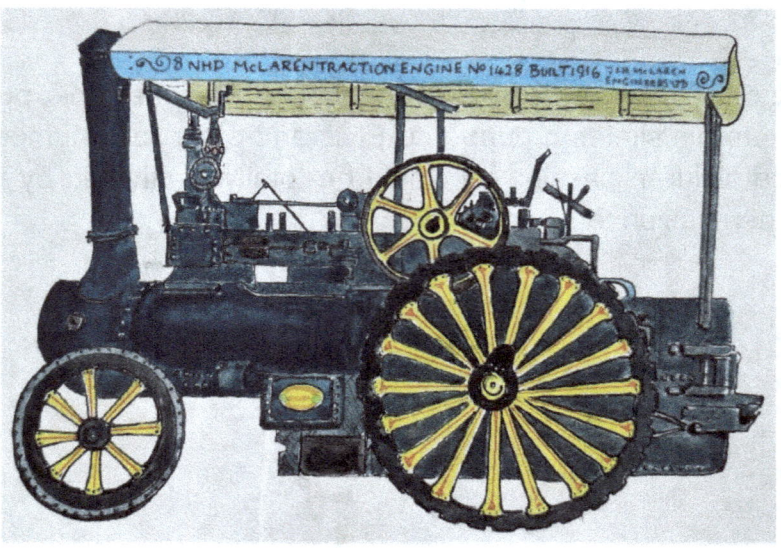

I have sketched around the Auckland Domain before (see the duck pond p45) but was struck by the lovely view looking between the lamp posts on the steps of the Domain which framed Rangitoto and North Head in the distance.

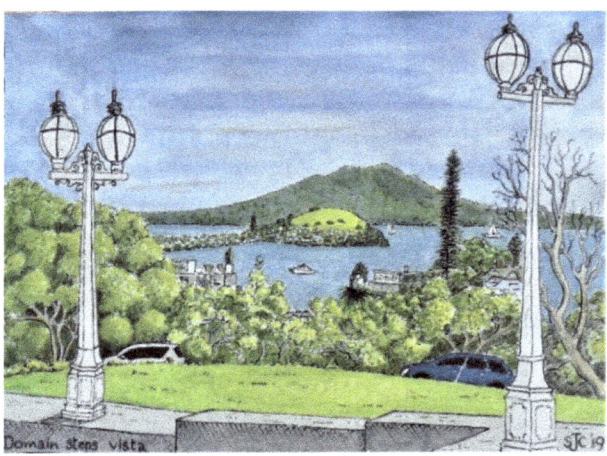

Devonport remains one of my favourite locations to sketch. It was one of the earliest settled areas of Auckland with a rich Māori and maritime history.

The volcanic mounts (Maunga) in the area were ideal for Māori Pā (fortified settlements) as they had quality soil and large tidal beaches for seafood harvesting. The Maunga were occupied by Māori from about 1350AD. Europeans started to settle in the area around the mid-1800s.

The following is a sketch looking up towards Mount Victoria (Takarunga) while sitting outside the library.

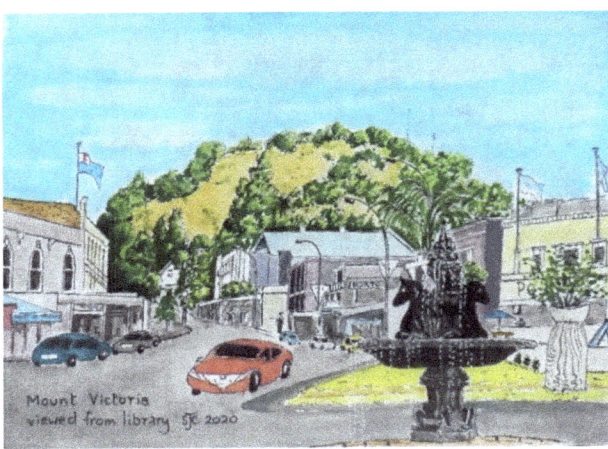

A walk along the prom takes you to Torpedo Bay, so-named because a section of land at the base of North Head was developed as a mine (known as torpedoes at that time) production site. For 3 years electro-contact mines were produced as defence but probably never deployed in the harbour. The site was eventually handed over to the Royal New Zealand Navy and in 2010 the associated National Museum was opened there. The following view is from the café looking back across the bay.

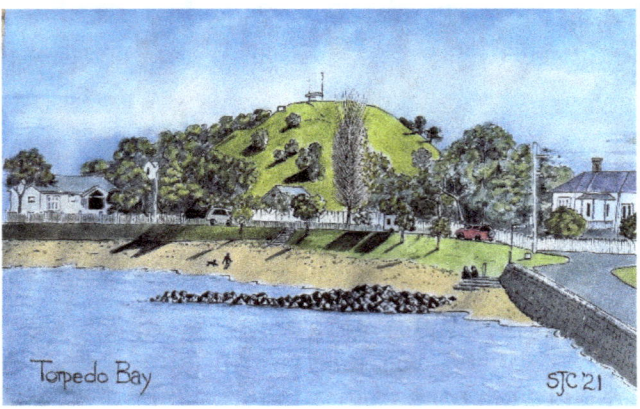

Another favourite site is Coxs Bay and a good view across to the Sea Scouts is from the bottom of Rawene Avenue.

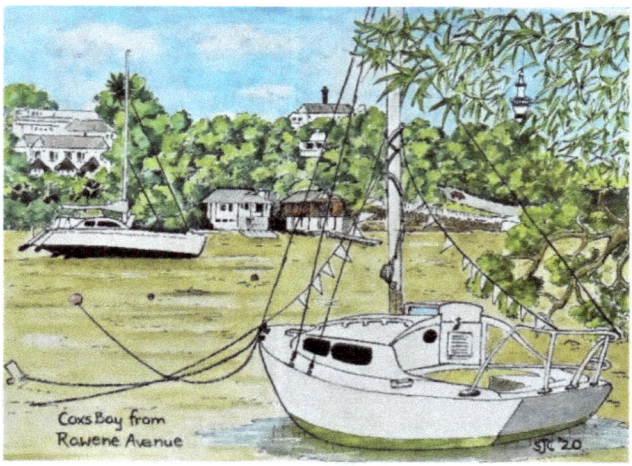

So picturesque I did it twice!

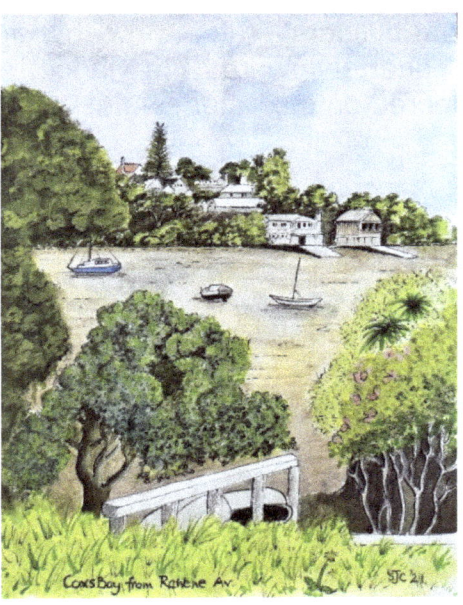

The Buoy Café still does a roaring trade and I still enjoy a 'flat white' and bacon and egg 'slider' sitting out on their deck area. The following is the view from the boardwalk looking back to the outside seating area.

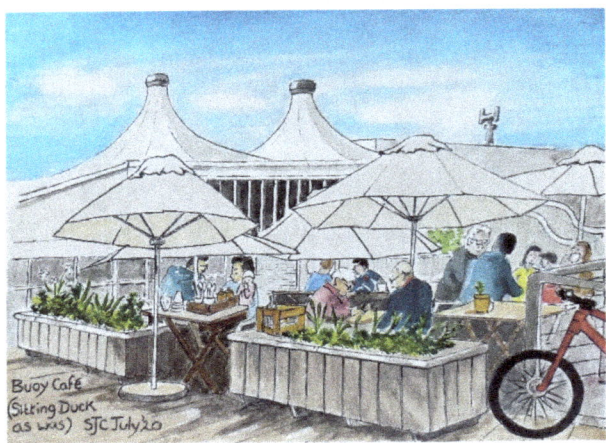

Heritage landing is located next to Silo Marina in Auckland's Wynyard quarter. It is the Classic Yacht Association's mooring. These historic wooden vessels showcase the maritime boat builders' craft and I came across it by chance while walking through Wynyard quarter towards the viaduct area. By contrast, there was a large superyacht moored on the other side of the landing nicely contrasting the old with the new.

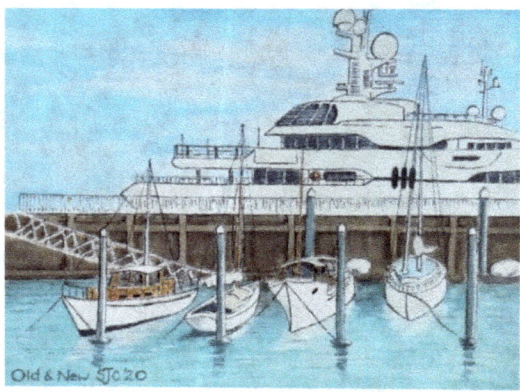

Sentinel beach is very close to where we live and is a good spot to set up a chair and have a relaxing read with a view out to the Harbour Bridge and Watchman Island. There are a number of boat sheds stretching out into the harbour but what you can't see tucked away on private land to the left of this picture is a helipad. I have just once experienced the draft of one such helicopter landing there.

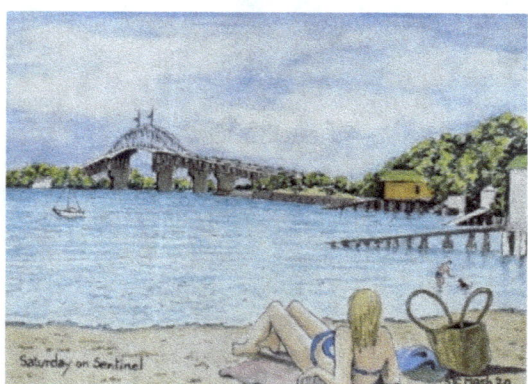

The outer link bus at the top of our road provides a good service around the city and if I want to visit the art galleries in Parnell I will use my AT Hop card for a free ride there.

I came across the following peaceful corner, with bench provided, tucked away off Parnell Rise. There is a bronze statue in memory of Les Harvey who was the creator of Parnell Village. It was just behind me on this multi-coloured brick path in the courtyard of Antoine's restaurant.

Harvey bought and restored a large dilapidated area in Parnell in the 1970s and established restaurants, craft shops and boutiques. He and other craftsmen were able to recycle salvaged bricks from demolished Victorian buildings and along with tree planting, garden development and old house conversions made Parnell Village what it is today.

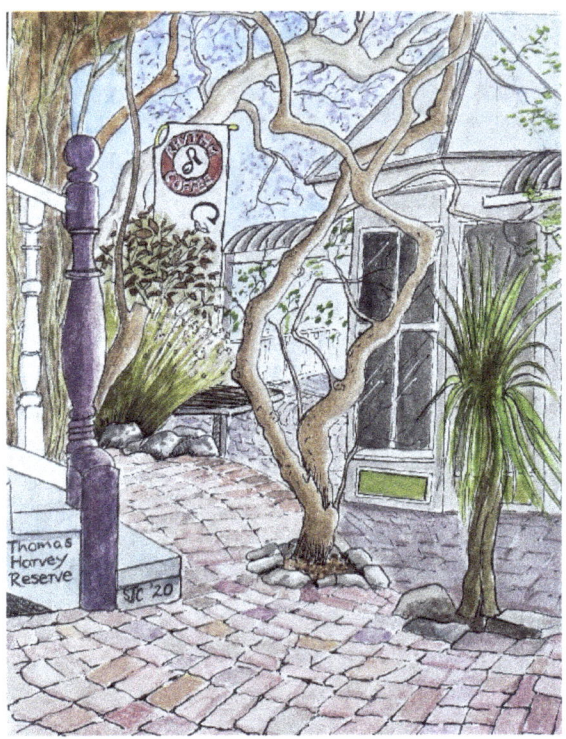

News started reporting that the Western Springs pine trees were going to be cut down by Auckland Council. The idea being to return the area to native bush with Kauri, Pūriri, Taraire and Tānekahe. The other rationale put forward for this was to remove a perceived risk to public safety and properties should the older pines start to fall.

There has been some local opposition but at this time of writing the plan looks to be going ahead. I thought I should sketch the pines before they disappeared and this was the result.

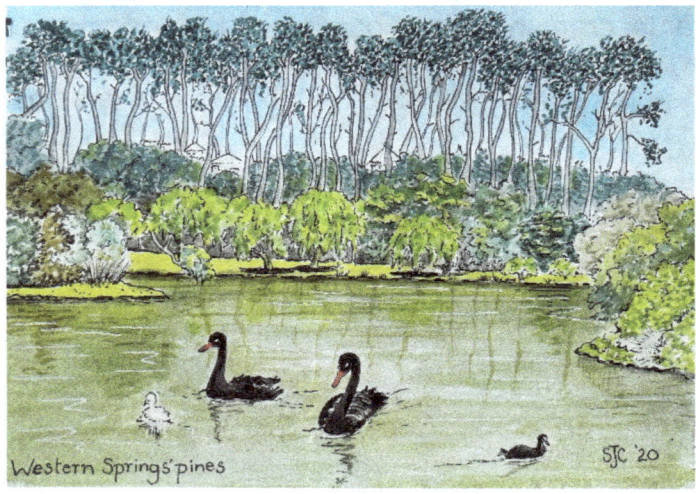

On a family trip to a bach in Omaha I spent an afternoon in Warkworth and came across two great spots to sketch along the river. The first one is Warkworth Wharf and in the foreground is one of Warkworth's steam boats, Kapanui, which was built in 1900. It is the only remaining one of three which takes passengers for trips down the Mahurangi river.

There is an interesting history of rivalry between the steam boats. The Kapanui and the Rose Casey collided while racing to pick up passengers and in 1905 the Kapanui was run down by the Claymore off Devonport Wharf and sank with five crew drowning. It was subsequently refloated and repaired.

Behind is moored the Jane Gifford which is New Zealand's only original scow which still sails. It was built in 1908 and would cart granite from mines in Coromandel to Auckland. She would have been one of some 130 scows that were used as water transport. Their flat bottoms would allow them to rest in an upright position even when the tide was out. This made it much easier to load freight and stock.

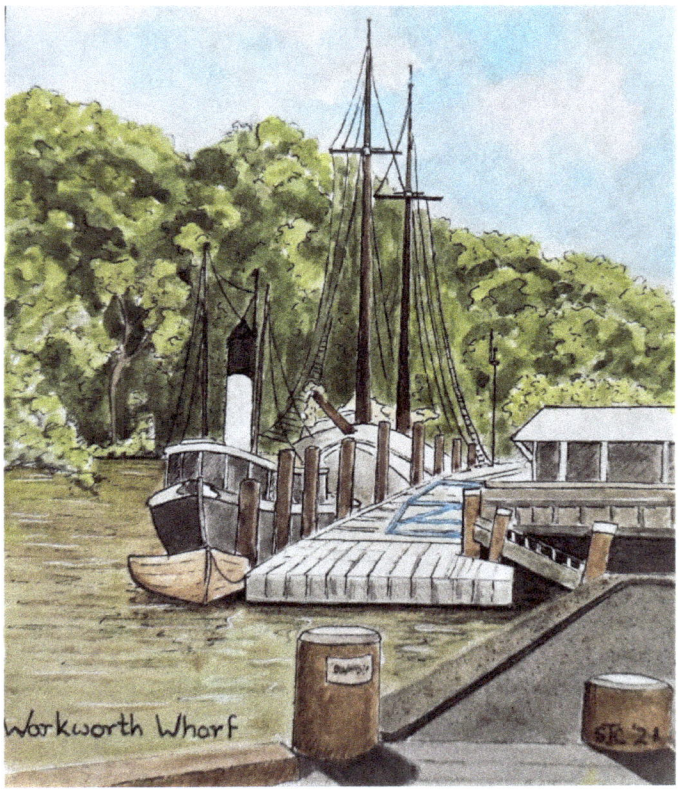

She was rebuilt and launched in 1992 but suffered some rot in the hull. In 2005 Warkworth residents purchased her and the restored vessel was finally relaunched in 2009 and is used for tourist trips, youth training, weddings and special events.

Tucked away at the side of the river close to the bridge in Warkworth was this picturesque spot.

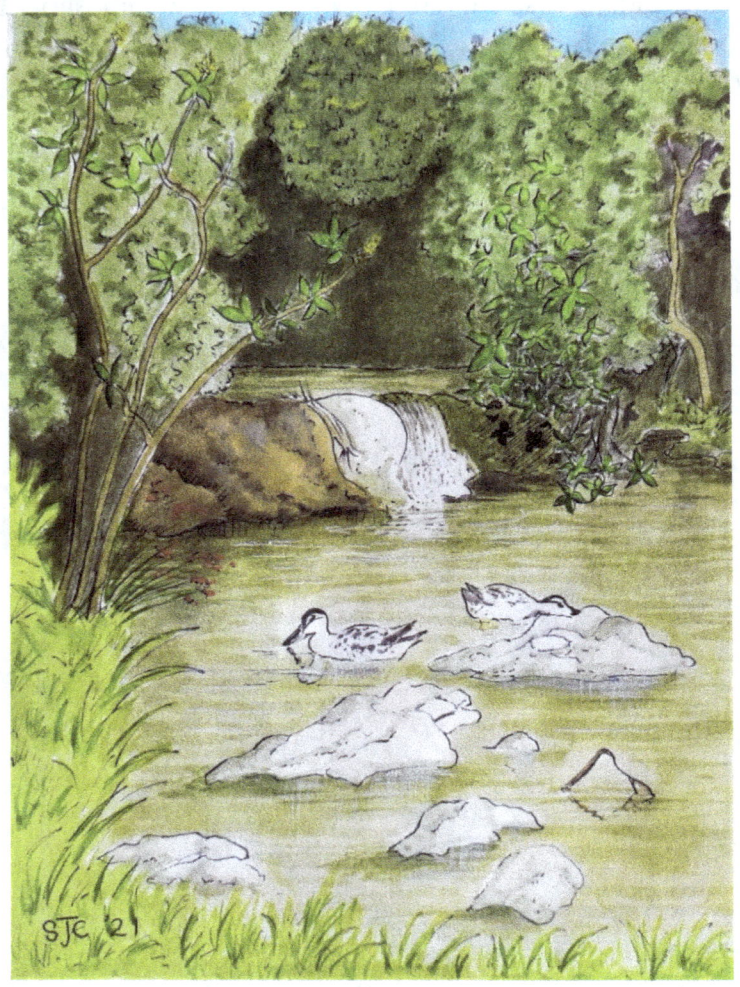

We subsequently spent a long weekend following the Whitianga art trail which was a great way to have access to a variety of artists in their home surroundings and a chance to see many examples of media including oils, watercolours, wood and glass.

Mercury Bay in Whitianga was a main timber exporting site in the 1830s. The wharf was first built in 1882.

The following view from the esplanade looks across the harbour to the Ferry Landing on the other side. The ferry between the two was established in 1895 and the wharf on the Ferry Landing side was built in 1837 from stone cut locally from cliffs and was the first to be built in Australasia.

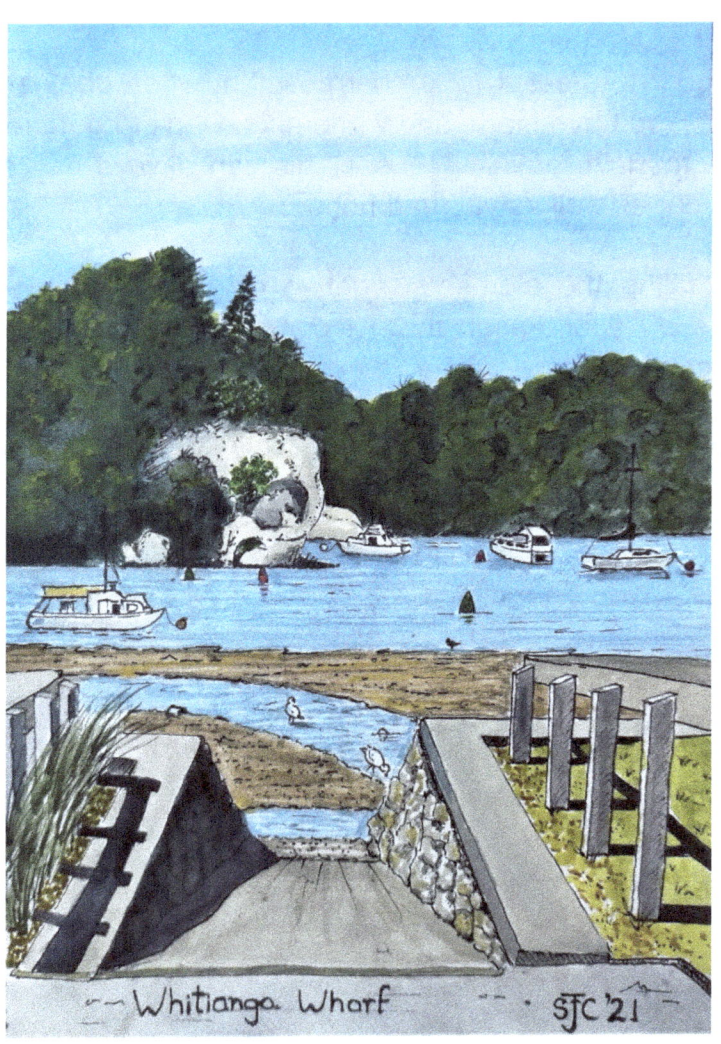

I can highly recommend taking a stroll/drive around your local neighbourhood and instead of taking a photograph of a picturesque scene just have a go at drawing what you see and if this works then splashing a bit of colour into it. By all means take a photograph as well, so that you can review the colour at a later stage. Apart from noting where shadows are falling on a sunny day and keeping their placement in your head, when sketching a bay, there is the added challenge of the receding tide to contend with.

You will conquer the feeling of embarrassment when people look over your shoulder once you have made a few attempts. Don't forget that the artist also has the right to claim artistic license! This can always be your excuse if it doesn't work out as well as you had hoped.

If you are battling the elements, fighting off bugs, grabbing your canvas before it flies off your easel, then a completed painting, at least to your satisfaction, can be a very enjoyable experience.

However, on a warm, windless, summer's day in the shade, what could be a better way of meditating than totally immersing yourself in the scenery and nature before you?

The End

All Sketched Out

ABOUT THE AUTHOR

Steve Connellan is a retired hospital doctor who has been fortunate enough to have the opportunity to rekindle his love for drawing and painting now that he has more time on his hands. Encouragement from his wife, extended New Zealand family and Plein Air Painters of NZ have ensured that he makes the most of the beautiful scenery on offer and will continue to do so until someone tells him it's time to stop!

As a spin off, he has tried his hand at illustrated children's short stories in verse.

These were stimulated by making up stories with his granddaughters and drawing pictures of the events as the story unfolded. These were called 'Drawry Stories'.

There are currently 7 in the 'Drawry Story' series available through Amazon books and authored by 'Grandpa':

Della the Daisy
The Frog Who Couldn't Whistle
The Lonely Spider
The Cheeky Little Yellow Car
The Blob
The Sneeze Saga
The Teeth Traveler

The Dog Who Tried To Talk (a children's chapter book - ISBN 9798734397497)

Medical publications include:

The Medical Tactician: A Century of Doctor-Patient Relationships (ISBN 1468163469)

Hives and Skin Swelling – A Simple Guide (ISBN 147743934X)

House Dust Mite – A Partnership for Life (ISBN 1495241106)

www.ingramcontent.com/pod-product-compliance
Lightning Source LLC
Chambersburg PA
CBHW080617220526
45466CB00010B/3364